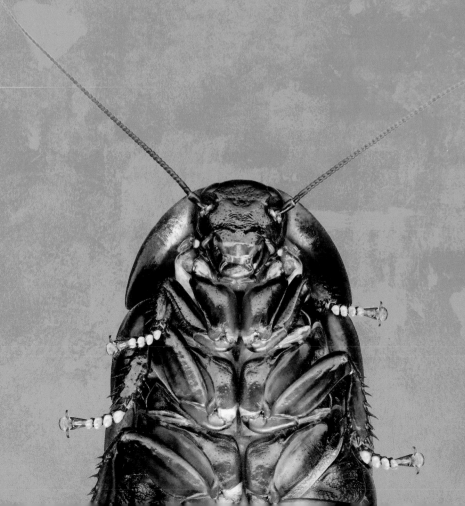

NATIONAL
GEOGRAPHIC
KiDS

DON'T READ THIS BOOK
Before Dinner

Revoltingly True Tales of
**FOUL FOOD, ICKY ANIMALS,
HORRIBLE HISTORY,**
and More

ANNA CLAYBOURNE

NATIONAL GEOGRAPHIC
WASHINGTON, D.C.

CONTENTS

PAGE 11

PAGE 55

PAGE 63

PAGE 134

DOES THE THOUGHT OF SEEING MAGGOTS MAKE YOU GIGGLE ... WITH GLEE? DO YOU DELIGHT IN HEARING **DISGUSTING FACTS** ABOUT GOOP, GUTS, OR GARBAGE? IF SO, YOU MIGHT JUST BE A FAN OF THE FOUL!

GETTING GROSSED OUT

Yeee-UCK! How many times have you thought that? Probably a lot. (Especially when you picked up this book and saw some of the pictures!) Feeling grossed out and disgusted is a very common, normal thing for us humans. It's often caused by things we encounter every day—even things from our own bodies, like spit and boogers. But why?

Disgust is not just an emotion—it is also a physical feeling. You might recoil and back away from whatever horrifying sight has grossed you out. If it's really bad, it can actually make you want to barf!

There are two main reasons this happens:

YOU'RE PROTECTING YOURSELF. People have an instinctual understanding that some types of gross things are not good for us. When you feel horrified by dog poop on the sidewalk and try to avoid it, your body is telling you to steer clear, because it really is full of dangerous germs.

YOU LEARNED IT. Humans have a bunch of facial expressions and noises for when we find something gross. *Ewwww! Yeuuuch! Bluergh! Aaaarrggh,* get it away from me!—and so on. As we're growing up, we pick up on these emotions whenever we hear and see other people reacting to things that disgust them. It gets so embedded in our brains that we might even feel grossed out by the same stuff.

For example, in most parts of the United States, people don't like the thought of eating a creepy-crawly, like a cricket or a tarantula (even if it's cooked!). Many people couldn't do it even if you paid them; they just find it too horrifying. Yet there's nothing scary or gross about eating bugs—it's a cultural fear that people learn from their environment.

In Cambodia, some types of insects and spiders are a normal part of people's diets. People there grow up learning that creepy-crawlies can be food, so they don't find ingesting insects gross at all.

However, most people from both those places will be grossed out by stinky smells and gruesome guts—showing that some things are basically revolting to all of us.

Prepare to Be Disgusted!

As you turn the page and read through this book, you're going to encounter a lot of truly revolting, gross, and gruesome things that really could turn your stomach! There's just so much disgusting stuff out there, including:

✿ Awful animals and putrid plants.

✿ Small but stomach-churning germs, mites, and other mini-monsters.

✿ Body bits—from boogers and blood to puke, poop, saliva, and sweat.

✿ Foods, flavors, and terrible smells that will make you go YUCK!

✿ The horrible habits of humans throughout history.

✿ Pesky pests and parasites that invade our homes or bodies.

✿ Medical missteps that won't make you feel better!

✿ Icky art, fashion, festivals, and other cultural creations that reveal just how fascinated we are with the disgusting, the revolting, and the creepy.

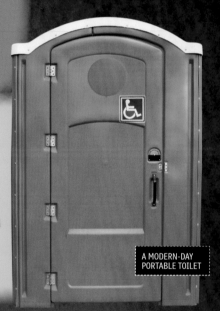

COCKROACHES CHOW DOWN ON AN APPLE.

GOING GAGA FOR GROSSNESS

So why would someone want to read a book full of repulsive stuff for fun? Strange as it may seem, some of us enjoy being horrified and grossed out—as long as it doesn't go too far.

It's similar to the way people enjoy horror stories and scary movies. As long as we know that we are really safe, experiencing fear—or gross-ness—makes us feel we're in control. Many people especially like sharing their grossed-out reactions and bonding over what makes them go *ewwww!* That's why you probably can't wait to freak out your mom or sibling by showing them a gross photo.

A MODERN-DAY PORTABLE TOILET

WARNING! GROSSNESS ALERT!

It is true that some people are extra sensitive to some of the gross things in this book—things like blood, wounds, vomit, or seeing human or animal insides.

✿ If that's you, proceed with caution! No one wants you puking all over the pages or passing out!

✿ If you're of a nervous disposition, maybe ask someone else to check out each page before you take a peek.

✿ Pay special attention to the yuck-o-meter at the top of each topic. It will give you a good idea of what you're dealing with, ranging from horrible but harmless to disastrously disgusting!

EWW GROSS NASTY DISGUSTING

YUCK-O-METER

OK, DON'T SAY WE HAVEN'T WARNED YOU. TAKE A DEEP BREATH, TURN THE PAGE, AND READ ON ... IF YOU DARE!

DECAYING DELICACIES

YUCK-O-METER

EWW · GROSS · NASTY · DISGUSTING

YOU OPEN THE REFRIGERATOR IN SEARCH OF A SNACK. MMM, LAST WEEK'S PIZZA? But HANG ON A MOMENT. You can't eat that … it's gone bad! At least, that's our usual reaction when we come across rotting food. And it's pretty smart too. Spoiled snacks can be seriously bad for your stomach. But guess what: There are some foods that people wait to eat until they're rotten—because that's how they like them! From lumps of smelly old shark meat to eggs buried in mud for months on end, decaying delicacies are popular around the world. To find out about them, hold your nose and read on.

THE ROTTEN HÁKARL IS HUNG OUT TO DRY.

HÁKARL MAY SEEM GROSS, BUT IT'S **ACTUALLY SAFER TO EAT** THAN FRESH GREENLAND SHARK! BEFORE THE FERMENTING PROCESS, THE SHARK'S MEAT IS **POISONOUS.**

HAVE SOME HÁKARL!

RECIPE: Take one Greenland shark (a big, slow-moving shark found in the Arctic), remove its head and guts, then bury it in sand. Pile on some rocks to really squash it down. Leave it there for a few weeks. Then dig it out and hang it up to dry. Several months later, cut the rotted shark into cubes and serve on toothpicks!

This is *kæstur hákarl* (pronounced KAI-stoor HOW-kadl), meaning "fermented shark," and it's a famous traditional snack in Iceland. It's also often described as the worst-tasting food in the world! The fermented, foul-smelling shark meat has a creamy, chewy texture and is said to REEK like a mixture of smelly socks, superstrong blue cheese, and bathroom bleach. The stench makes many people's eyes water, and some can't help gagging when they put it in their mouth!

So why do people in Iceland like it? Well, actually, many of them don't. Hákarl originated as a way to preserve shark meat for a long time, before the days of refrigerators. These days, it's more popular among tourists, who like to try it as a dare, though some people do have a taste for it.

MOLDY, MUSHY CORN

No farmer wants to find gross gray mold growing all over their corn crop. Except for some farmers in Mexico, where corn mold is collected and cooked up as a tasty treat! It's called *huitlacoche* (pronounced weet-la-KOTSH-eh), and though no one knows the exact translation, it is said to come from the Aztec people's word for "raven poop" or "sleeping poop." Once fried, the corn mold becomes a blackened mush that people eat in stews, tacos, or tamales. It's said to have a delicious earthy flavor. In fact, it's so popular that farmers can sell it for a higher price than their non-moldy corn!

In other countries, farmers usually try to get rid of corn mold. But this is changing, as huitlacoche is now becoming a trend in some of the fanciest restaurants.

CORN TAKEN OVER BY THE MONSTER MOLD

HOW IS THAT SAFE?

WE ALL KNOW ROTTEN FOOD CAN MAKE YOU SICK—SO HOW ARE THESE FOODS SAFE? IT'S ALL ABOUT THE DIFFERENCE BETWEEN ROTTING AND FERMENTATION. ROTTING HAPPENS WHEN BACTERIA, MOLD, OR FUNGI GET INTO FOOD AND BREAK IT DOWN. FERMENTATION IS THE SAME, BUT IT USES ONLY PARTICULAR BACTERIA OR MOLDS THAT ARE OK TO EAT. MANY EVERYDAY FOODS, LIKE YOGURT, BREAD, AND CHEESE, ARE MADE THROUGH THE PROCESS OF FERMENTATION.

ANCIENT EGGS?

The eggs here certainly look like they could be a century old. But don't worry—they're actually only a few months past their sell-by date! These black, shiny morsels are called century eggs, a popular Chinese snack sometimes known as "horse pee eggs" thanks to their smell.

The eggs are prepared by covering raw duck, chicken, or quail eggs in a mixture of ash, salt, black tea, and lime. Over several weeks or months, the egg yolks become a greenish black cheesy substance, while the whites turn to jelly. They're eaten with pickled ginger or rice porridge, most often at parties.

ERRIBLE TOILETS

NASTY

DISGUSTING

...-O-METER

WHEN YOU GOTTA GO, YOU GOTTA GO! And that means we have to "go" somewhere. Fortunately, most modern bathrooms have a flushing toilet that carries away all that icky waste. But it wasn't always this way …

MODERN FLUSHING TOILETS WEREN'T INVENTED UNTIL 1596, BY JOHN HARINGTON, A GODSON OF QUEEN ELIZABETH I OF ENGLAND. IT MAY BE THANKS TO HIM THAT A TOILET IS SOMETIMES CALLED A JOHN!

GARDYLOO!

If you were walking down the street a few hundred years ago and you heard a warning like "Gardyloo!" or "Look out below!" you'd get out of the way—fast! This meant that someone was about to empty their waste out their window, right into the street.

Before about 200 years ago, most homes didn't have a toilet. Instead, people did their business in a large bowl called a chamber pot, which they kept under their bed. When it was full, out the window it went! As you can imagine, the streets in those days were pretty stinky. Many cities eventually banned the emptying of chamber pots into the street. Instead, you had to head to the nearest river.

CLOSE-STOOL TOILET

A FANCY CHAMBER POT FROM THE 1700s

IN THE PAST, PEOPLE WOULD THROW THE CONTENTS OF THEIR CHAMBER POTS OUT WINDOWS.

PORTABLE PRIVIES

Some people, especially in the countryside, had an outdoor bathroom, called an outhouse or a privy. It was built over a pit dug in the ground and featured a plank with a hole in it as a seat. Over time, the pit filled up with waste. Then people simply moved their privy somewhere else. In fact, privies—now often called portable toilets—are still used today. They can be found in many parts of the world and are often seen at campsites and festivals.

DON'T SWIM IN THE MOAT!

If you were lucky enough to live in a castle in medieval Europe, between 500 and 1,000 years ago, you might have had your own en suite toilet built into the bedroom wall. These toilets, called garderobes, had a hole that led to the outside of the castle. From there, human waste dropped straight down into the castle moat. Of course, this made the moat smell seriously bad—all the better for discouraging enemies who might want to get across it!

HELP—THERE'S NO TOILET PAPER!

... BECAUSE IT HASN'T BEEN INVENTED YET! SO WHAT DID PEOPLE USE TO WIPE WITH IN TIMES GONE BY?

LEAVES: THE OBVIOUS CHOICE FOR COUNTRY FOLK, AND PROBABLY POPULAR IN PREHISTORIC TIMES TOO.

MOSS: MOSS IS NICE AND SOFT, AND USEFUL IN FAR NORTHERN LANDS, WHERE THERE ARE FEWER LEAFY TREES AND PLANTS.

SNOW: *BRRRRR!* FOR THE INUIT AND OTHER PEOPLE IN VERY COLD AREAS, A HANDFUL OF SNOW WAS THE TRADITIONAL METHOD.

STONES: OUCH! SOME ANCIENT GREEKS USED STONE OR CLAY PEBBLES, CALLED *PESSOI.*

OLD BOOKS: *THE OLD FARMER'S ALMANAC,* A YEARLY CALENDAR AND REFERENCE BOOK, FIRST APPEARED IN 1792 IN NORTH AMERICA. IT CAME WITH A HOLE THROUGH ONE CORNER SO YOU COULD HANG IT UP IN THE PRIVY TO USE AS TOILET PAPER (ONCE

ANCIENT AMENITIES

Some ancient civilizations actually had fairly sophisticated toilets. As long as 5,000 years ago, the people of the Indus Valley civilization (in what is now Pakistan) built brick toilets in their homes. Each toilet led to an underground sewer, very similar to modern plumbing today. After using one, people emptied a jug of water into it to wash everything away. This was probably the first version of a flushing toilet system in history.

The Romans had "flushing" toilets too, with seats built over a ditch filled with running water. The seats were arranged all together in rows, though, so it wasn't very private!

SLOBBERY SPIT

YOU HAVE IT IN YOUR MOUTH ALL THE TIME. YOU EVEN SWALLOW IT REGULARLY. So there can't be anything that gross about spit … can there? For many people, spitting is one of the most revolting, disgusting, and downright rude things you can possibly do. When spit is in our bodies, it's fine. But once it's out—eww!

DRIBBLING DROOL

INSIDE YOUR MOUTH, THERE ARE SEVERAL MINI-ORGANS CALLED SALIVARY GLANDS. In a typical day, they squirt out around four cups (1 L) of saliva, or spit. It's mostly made of water but also contains a bunch of chemicals that make it extra thick, slimy, and stringy! That could be one reason we find it so gross.

Healthy spit isn't harmful, but when you have a cold or the flu, your spit is full of germs. You might cough up green, gloopy phlegm and spit it out, or spray it around when you sneeze. That means other people could touch the germs or breathe them in.

So it's no wonder that spitting on the ground—or even worse, at another person—is seen as seriously scuzzy. In fact, scientists have even done experiments where they asked people to spit into a glass of water and then take a sip. They didn't want to! Even their own spit grossed them out.

IF YOU DON'T LIKE THE SIGHT OF **SLOBBER**, AVOID KEEPING A MASTIFF AS A PET. THIS DROOLY DOG SHAKES ITS HEAD AND SPLATTERS ITS **DRIPPING DRIBBLE** ALL OVER THE PLACE.

IF YOU SNEEZE WITHOUT COVERING YOUR MOUTH AND NOSE, A FINE SPRAY OF SPIT SHOOTS OUT.

DON'T STAND TOO CLOSE!

NO SPITTING ALLOWED!

SPITTING IS SOMETIMES ACCEPTABLE IN SOME COUNTRIES AND CULTURES. In Singapore, a country in Asia, and in Barcelona, Spain, for example, spitting in the street could land you with a fine—while among the Maasai people of Kenya, Africa, it's a way to be friendly and polite. Sports players often spit, because running around a lot can generate extra saliva. And of course, babies are allowed to dribble!

SPIT SOUP

BIRD'S NEST SOUP

ONE TYPE OF BIRD, THE EDIBLE-NEST SWIFTLET FROM SOUTHEAST ASIA, ACTUALLY MAKES ITS NEST OUT OF ITS OWN SALIVA.
It dribbles a little saliva onto a cave wall or cliff face, and the saliva dries and hardens. Gradually the swift adds more and more saliva to build up a cup-shaped nest of hardened spit for its babies to sit in.
But it gets grosser: Some people prize the crusty saliva as a food, so they collect the old nests, soak them in water, and cook them to make a traditional delicacy, bird's nest soup. According to people who eat it, it doesn't taste like much but is satisfyingly slimy and gelatinous.

THERE ARE CONTESTS AND OFFICIAL RECORDS FOR SPITTING CHERRY STONES, AND ALSO CRICKETS (YES, THAT'S SPITTING A DEAD CRICKET).

NO SPIT, NO FLAVOR!

TRY THIS NOT-SO-TASTY TWO-MINUTE EXPERIMENT. If you dry your tongue all over with a piece of paper towel and then put a salty potato chip on it, you'll probably taste nothing at all! You need a good layer of saliva on your tongue to help your taste buds work.

A SLOBBERY TONGUE MIGHT SEEM GROSS, BUT IT HAS ITS USES!

SPIT SCIENCE

IT MAY BE SLOBBERY AND SLIMY, BUT SALIVA IS SUPER USEFUL AND DOES SEVERAL IMPORTANT JOBS:

❀ It mixes with food to make it soft and mushy, so it's easier to chew and swallow. That's why your mouth waters at the sight of yummy food—you're getting ready to munch!

❀ It washes food into the taste buds on your tongue, so you can taste it.

❀ It contains chemicals called enzymes that break down food and start to digest it, even before it reaches your stomach.

❀ It dissolves food that's stuck between your teeth, helping to keep them clean. That's why chewing gum can be good for your teeth—it makes your mouth release extra saliva.

CREEPY-CRAWLY COCKROACHES

FLATTENED, OVAL BODY

TEENY HEAD

YUCK-O-METER

EWW · GROSS · NASTY · DISGUSTING

IMAGINE OPENING A FOOD CUPBOARD OR A PACKAGE OF COOKIES and suddenly finding a big, shiny, beetlelike bug with hairy legs and long, spindly antennae. ICK— it's a cockroach!

Even though these critters don't sting and rarely bite, many people find cockroaches so horrifying that the sight of one makes them scream, drop everything, and run. So what is it that makes cockroaches so creepy and revolting?

VERY LONG ANTENNAE, OR FEELERS

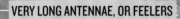

DINNER GUESTS

Cockroaches munch on our leftovers, garbage, stored food, and any crumbs left lying around. And wherever they go, they bring dirt and germs. They hide under floors, in trash cans, and around rotting food, droppings, mold, and bacteria. Dirt sticks to their feet and bodies and spreads all over whatever they eat. If there are cockroaches in your cookie jar, you're not going to want to eat those cookies! (And even if cockroach-covered cookies don't bother you, you could get a nasty case of food poisoning from eating them.)

THERE ARE OVER 4,600 DIFFERENT TYPES, OR SPECIES, OF COCKROACHES. ONLY A SMALL NUMBER OF THESE—ABOUT 30— INVADE OUR HOMES.

POOP PICNIC

Roaches prefer real food, but they're not fussy. They'll eat anything to survive, and that includes rotting meat, dead leaves, human skin and hair, glue, soap, paper, leather, each other ... and, yes, poop.

REEKING ROACHES

Cockroaches also give off their own special, stinky smell—a musty, moldy, oily odor that's a dead giveaway that the tiny terrors are lurking nearby. And the more roaches you have hiding in your home, the stronger the stench will be.

Eau de cockroach is made up of a variety of gross ingredients, including:

- Cockroach spit, which is released as the bugs chew on their food (your food, that is!).
- Smelly chemicals that the roaches release from their bodies to signal to one another.
- Cockroach poop. Cockroaches aren't tidy creatures. They just poop anywhere.
- Dead roaches that have started to decay.

TO REACH THEIR **TOP SPEED**, COCKROACHES GET UP AND SPRINT USING THEIR **TWO HIND LEGS**, JUST LIKE HUMANS!

RAPID ROACHES

Cockroaches are known for their amazing high-speed running skills. In fact, they are among the fastest runners of the insect world. American cockroaches, one of the most common species, have been clocked running at five feet per second, or 3.4 miles an hour (5 km/h). That's faster than the typical human walks, and cockroaches are much smaller than humans. If a cockroach were the size of a human (don't think about that too much!), it could run at more than 200 miles an hour (322 km/h)—faster than an express train.

BROWN, SHINY SURFACE

LONG, HAIRY LEGS

SUPER SURVIVORS

IF YOU THINK YOU'RE GETTING RID OF THOSE PESKY ROACHES, BE WARNED: IT'S NOT THAT EASY! THEY'RE FAMOUS FOR THEIR ABILITY TO SURVIVE ALMOST ANYTHING. BUT IS IT TRUE? HERE ARE FIVE TOUGH SURVIVAL TESTS. CAN A COCKROACH PASS THEM?

- ☑ **WATER:** A COCKROACH CAN SURVIVE BEING UNDERWATER FOR AS LONG AS 30 MINUTES—MUCH LONGER THAN A HUMAN CAN.

- ☑ **HEADLESSNESS:** A COCKROACH CAN SURVIVE FOR A WEEK AFTER LOSING ITS HEAD. ROACHES BREATHE THROUGH HOLES IN THEIR SKIN, SO THEY WON'T RUN OUT OF OXYGEN, EVEN WITHOUT A MOUTH. THEY CAN MANAGE WITHOUT FOOD FOR A MONTH, BUT THEY WILL DIE WITHOUT A DRINK OF WATER AFTER ABOUT ONE WEEK.

- ☑ **A GIANT ASTEROID:** COCKROACHES HAVE EXISTED FOR A LONG TIME—OVER 320 MILLION YEARS. AROUND 65 MILLION YEARS AGO, AN ASTEROID STRIKE WIPED OUT THE DINO- SAURS, BUT THE ROACHES KEPT GOING ...

- ☒ **NUCLEAR ARMAGEDDON:** COCKROACHES ARE SAID TO BE ABLE TO WITHSTAND A NUCLEAR EXPLOSION, BUT IT'S NOT REALLY TRUE. HOWEVER, THEY CAN SURVIVE ABOUT 10 TIMES MORE RADIATION THAN HUMANS CAN.

- ☒ **A BIG BOOT:** THERE ARE BEETLES, LIKE THE SUPER-TOUGH- SHELLED IRONCLAD BEETLE, THAT CAN SURVIVE BEING SQUASHED. BUT A COCKROACH CAN'T.

WORLD'S WORST SMELLS

GROSS NASTY
EWW DISGUSTING
YUCK-O-METER

WHAT'S THE WORST SMELL YOU'VE EVER EXPERIENCED?
A really bad smell—and we mean really, really bad—can actually make you gag, throw up, or even faint. A terrible stink can ruin a restaurant or hotel, make people move out of their home, or even be used as a weapon!
We've rounded up some of the world's most obscene odors and foul funks to find out which are the most awful of all. Hold your nose!

SOMETHING'S FISHY!

Ask people what the worst thing they've ever smelled is, and rotting fish will be pretty high up on the list. In fact, it's not just fish: Most sea creatures, including squid, crabs, whales, and shellfish, tend to stink. They all have that distinct scent that can only be described as "fishy," especially when they've died and have begun to break down.

The reason sea creatures smell that way is because their bodies contain a chemical that stops them from soaking up too much salt from the sea (which would be bad for them). After they die, this chemical breaks down into a different substance, called trimethylamine, or TMA. It's the TMA that really starts to stink after a few days.

ICKY ISLAND

Seal Island, near the coast of South Africa, is said to be one of the smelliest places you can possibly set foot on. Imagine the stink of a garbage can full of dead fish, mix in a pile of poop, and multiply it all by a thousand! The island is tiny—only five acres (2 ha)—but home to more than 60,000 seals ... as well as their piles of fish-filled poop and the rotting dead fish they haven't gotten around to eating yet. There's also a host of seabirds and their stinky fish poop too. Tourists like to go wildlife-spotting there, but most can't stand the smell for long!

SEAL ISLAND, SOUTH AFRICA

VILE VOLCANO

Another contender for smelliest spot is Ijen volcano, in Indonesia. It constantly passes gases from underground that are full of sulfur, an incredibly foul-smelling mineral that stinks of rotten eggs, toilets, and socks. Just going near the volcano makes your eyes water and your throat sting. So spare a thought for the sulfur miners, who walk up and down the slopes several times each day to chip off chunks of valuable sulfur—with only a small cloth to protect their noses!

WORKERS MINE SULFUR IN IJEN VOLCANO IN INDONESIA.

ONE OF THE GASES THAT MAKE IJEN VOLCANO SMELL SO BAD IS HYDROGEN SULFIDE. THIS SAME GAS IS ALSO FOUND IN ROTTEN EGGS AND IN THE SMELLY HUMAN GAS THAT ESCAPES FROM OUR INSIDES!

HUMAN-MADE STENCHES

SOME SCIENTISTS ACTUALLY SPEND THEIR DAYS CREATING EYE-WATERINGLY OBNOXIOUS ODORS. HERE ARE JUST A FEW OF THEM ...

ETHYL MERCAPTAN: THIS STINKY LIQUID SMELLS LIKE RAW ONIONS AND STINKY SOCKS. YOU CAN DETECT A WHIFF OF IT EVEN IF THERE'S ONLY ONE PART OF IT IN A BILLION PARTS OF AIR. IT'S A HELPFUL SMELL, THOUGH; IT'S ADDED TO DANGEROUS GASES TO HELP PEOPLE SPOT GAS LEAKS.

STENCH SOUP: THIS IS A SMELL WEAPON DEVELOPED BY TOP SMELL SCIENTIST PAMELA DALTON, USING ODORS OF POOP, ROTTING MEAT, AND SULFUR (THAT GOOD OLD ROTTEN-EGG SMELL). A SMELL LIKE THIS COULD BE USED TO MAKE ENEMIES RUN FOR COVER.

WHO, ME?: A STRANGE SCENT CODE-NAMED "WHO, ME?" WAS INVENTED IN THE UNITED STATES DURING THE SECOND WORLD WAR TO BE USED AGAINST ENEMY ARMY OFFICERS. IT WAS DESIGNED TO BE SPRAYED ON THE VICTIM TO MAKE THEM SMELL LIKE POOP! THE IDEA WAS THAT THE STINKY OFFICER WOULD FEEL EMBARRASSED AND LOSE RESPECT. HOWEVER, IT NEVER REALLY WORKED. IT WAS IMPOSSIBLE TO SPRAY THE STENCH WITHOUT GETTING YOURSELF

WAFTING WEASEL BUTT

Yes, you read that right. Another smell that's reported to be truly unbearable is the rancid reek of a weasel's rear end! Like other mammals, including tigers, dogs, and bears, weasels have glands near their behinds called anal glands. When the animal poops, the glands release a smelly substance that mixes with the poop. It's usually a way of marking the animal's territory to warn other animals to stay away.

In some weasels, though, the smelly stuff is extra strong. Instead of marking territory, it's used as a defense to fend off predators. It smells disgusting when the weasel is alive. When a weasel dies and decays, it smells even worse—something like a mixture of dead rotting fish, diarrhea, and coal tar.

DINNER IS SERVED!

GROSS NASTY DISGUSTING EWW

YUCK-O-METER

THESE DAYS, IF YOU GO TO A FANCY RESTAURANT FOR DINNER, YOU COULD BE RISKING AN OFF-PUTTING EXPERIENCE WHEN THE FOOD ARRIVES. Will it be on a plate? Or could it turn up on some other object—like a slab of rock, a table tennis racket, or an old skateboard?

Restaurants have recently begun dreaming up all kinds of original, eye-catching, and sometimes slightly icky ways to present their wares. Why? Well, doing something different is a way for a restaurant to stand out—especially in the age of social media, when people like to take photos of their meals and post them online. The weirder the picture, the more likely it is to be shared, giving the restaurant extra publicity.

Super cool or super disgusting? Here are just a few of the weirdest, grossest, and strangest examples!

SHOE SHOCKER

UNLESS YOU WERE RAISED BY WOLVES, YOUR PARENTS PROBABLY TAUGHT YOU THAT SHOES DO NOT GO ON THE DINNER TABLE. As your shoes schlep around on the ground outdoors, they can pick up all kinds of dirt and germs. In fact, many people find them so gross, they won't even wear shoes indoors ... let alone use them as plates.

Well, that rule has gone out the window now! French fries, battered tempura, and potato croquettes have all been served up nestled inside a high-heeled shoe or a sneaker. One top restaurant presented diners with their dessert on a rubber flip-flop. Another dished up bread rolls for the table inside a fluffy slipper (at least it probably kept them warm!).

HOSPITAL **HORROR**

MOST PEOPLE PROBABLY DON'T WANT TO BE REMINDED OF HOSPITALS, OPERATIONS, OR DISEASES AT THE DINNER TABLE. Even so, medical equipment is a popular theme at certain cafés. Drinks come in large syringes, which you are supposed to squirt into your mouth. Sometimes squishy foods, such as soup or guacamole, do too. A more substantial main course might even appear in a shiny metal medical bowl, or even be made to look like body parts!

SQUEAMISH THEMES

CHECK OUT THESE GROSS-THEMED EATERIES FROM AROUND THE WORLD!
MODERN TOILET, TAIWAN
THIS POPULAR ASIAN RESTAURANT CHAIN HAS A BATHROOM AND TOILET THEME. YOU SIT ON A TOILET-STYLE CHAIR, EAT FROM A TOILET BOWL, AND DRINKS ARE SERVED IN A MINI-URINAL!
BODY BAKERY, THAILAND
IN 2003, THAI ART STUDENT KITTIWAT UNARROM BEGAN USING HIS PARENTS' BAKERY TO MAKE BREAD SHAPED AND DECORATED TO LOOK LIKE HUMAN HEADS AND OTHER BODY PARTS. THEY ARE SAID TO TASTE GREAT!
POOP CAFÉ, CANADA
THE POOP CAFÉ IN TORONTO, CANADA, IS THEMED AROUND THE POPULAR "PILE OF POOP" EMOJI. AS WELL AS POOP EMOJI DECOR, AND SOUP SERVED IN TOILET-SHAPED BOWLS, IT HAS POOP-EMOJI-SHAPED MERINGUES (DESSERTS MADE FROM EGG WHITES AND SUGAR).

GROSS GARDEN TOOLS

DON'T GET US WRONG—GARDENS ARE GREAT. STILL, DIRT IS ... WELL ... DIRTY, AND PACKED WITH BILLIONS OF GERMS. When you think of garden shovels and flowerpots, you might even imagine them in a damp, dingy shed, covered in snails and spiderwebs.

Yet spades and shovels are very popular as replacement serving "dishes." You can have a cooked breakfast, a noodle stir-fry, or a slice of chocolate cake served on a shovel. Some restaurants also continue the theme with fries served in a flowerpot, and sauces or drinks in watering cans.

IS IT **CLEAN?**

DESPITE THE UNUSUAL SERVING STYLES, RESTAURANTS HAVE SUPER-STRICT HYGIENE RULES. If your dinner is served on a shoe or a shovel, it's probably new, sparkling clean, and hasn't actually been used to dig out weeds or pound the pavement. But people still get grossed out because of the way our brains associate one thing with another. If you can't help thinking about earthworms or dog poop, you could soon lose your appetite!

EVEN MORE CRAZY CONCEPTS REPORTED BY RESTAURANT-GOERS HAVE INCLUDED FOOD SERVED IN DOG BOWLS, ON FLOOR TILES, ON REAL RAT TRAPS, AND EVEN ON A BUNDLE OF BARBED WIRE!

POOP-SHAPED MERINGUES ... YUM!

REPULSIVE REMEDIES

YUCK-O-METER

EWW · GROSS · NASTY · DISGUSTING

DON'T TRY THIS AT HOME!

FOR PEOPLE WHO LIVED LONG AGO, GETTING SICK WAS SERIOUSLY BAD NEWS. Whether it was a headache, a toothache, or a dose of the Black Death, your doctor would probably try a medical treatment that would be horribly painful, disgustingly gross, or usually a combination of both!

BAD BLOOD

As you probably know, blood is a pretty important part of your body. You need it to stay alive, and you can't afford to lose too much of it.

However, the ancient Greeks thought that blood was one of four body substances, called the humors, that had to be in balance. (The others were the gross-sounding yellow bile, black bile, and phlegm.) All kinds of illnesses were blamed on having too much blood, making the body "out of balance."

So, right up until the 1800s, bloodletting—that is, letting some blood out—was a common "cure" for things like headaches, fevers, anxiety, and even heart attacks. The doctor would simply cut a small hole in the patient's arm (or sometimes even their neck). Blood would spurt out and the doctor would catch it in a bowl.

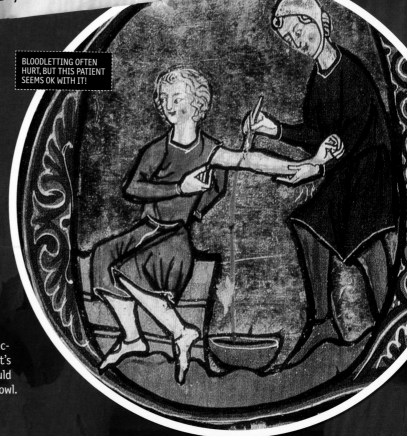

BLOODLETTING OFTEN HURT, BUT THIS PATIENT SEEMS OK WITH IT!

POOPY POTIONS

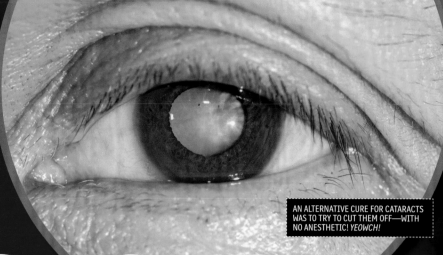

Animal poop, and even human poop, has been used in medicines since ancient times. Find out what kind of poop was used for which complaint with our handy guide.

 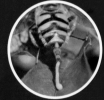   

SPLINTERS:
DONKEY POOP

The Ebers Papyrus, an ancient Egyptian scroll full of medical tips, says a splinter should be treated by covering it with donkey poop.

CRYING BABY:
FLY POOP

Another ancient Egyptian recipe involved scraping fly poop off the wall, mixing it into a drink, and giving it to babies to stop them from crying.

BALDNESS:
CHICKEN POOP

A book from the 1600s called *The Path-Way to Health* suggested washing your bald head with chicken droppings to make the hair grow back.

NOSEBLEED:
PIG POOP

Also in the 1600s, one cure for a nosebleed was to stuff some pig dung up your nose.

CATARACTS:
HUMAN POOP

A cataract is a condition that makes the lens of your eye cloud over. Seventeenth-century scientist Robert Boyle had the answer: Dry human poop into a powder and sprinkle it into the affected eye!

MOLDY MIRACLE

THE ANCIENT EGYPTIANS HAD A VERY WEIRD-SOUNDING BUT EFFECTIVE TREATMENT FOR SMALL INJURIES. IF YOU CUT YOUR HAND OR SCRAPED YOUR KNEE, YOU SIMPLY SLAPPED A SLICE OF OLD, MOLDY BREAD ONTO IT AS A KIND OF BANDAGE. IT SOUNDS YUCKY, BUT IT TURNS OUT THE EGYPTIANS HAD ACTUALLY DISCOVERED A BASIC FORM OF ANTIBIOTICS THOUSANDS OF YEARS BEFORE MODERN DOCTORS BEGAN USING THEM.

ANTIBIOTICS ARE GERM-KILLING CHEMICALS THAT ARE SOMETIMES MADE BY CERTAIN TYPES OF MOLD. SO THE MOLDY BREAD PROBABLY DID HELP TO DISINFECT WOUNDS AND SPEED UP HEALING. IT WASN'T UNTIL 1928 THAT SCOTTISH SCIENTIST ALEXANDER FLEMING DISCOVERED THE SAME THING IN HIS SCIENCE LAB, AND ANTIBIOTICS IN PILL FORM BECAME A PART OF MODERN MEDICINE.

WHEN A DISEASE CALLED THE PLAGUE, OR BLACK DEATH, STRUCK EUROPE, DOCTORS BELIEVED IT WAS CAUSED BY CLOUDS OF POISONOUS AIR FLOATING AROUND. SO THEY TOLD PEOPLE TO PASS GAS INTO A JAR, AND WAFT IT AROUND WHEN THEY WERE NEAR PLAGUE VICTIMS, TO FIGHT OFF THE BAD AIR!

THE DIRT ON DOO-DOO

YUCK-O-METER
EWW · GROSS · NASTY · DISGUSTING

EVERYONE DOES IT … POOP, THAT IS! But why? It's icky and nasty, right? But it's also totally necessary. Read on to learn why you should be glad to go number 2!

Better Out THAN IN!

Pooping is your body's way of getting rid of waste: undigested food, germs, dead cells, mucus, and smelly body chemicals.

Poop, also known as feces, is made in your digestive system, a long sequence of tubes and organs that runs all the way through your body. You use this system to eat and digest food to give your body energy and other useful things it needs. By the time the food has made its way through, and had all the useful bits taken out, poop is what remains. If you didn't have a system for dumping it out at the other end, it would build up inside you!

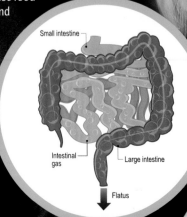

Small intestine

Intestinal gas

Large intestine

Flatus

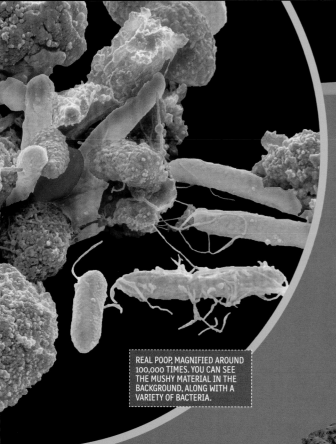

REAL POOP, MAGNIFIED AROUND 100,000 TIMES. YOU CAN SEE THE MUSHY MATERIAL IN THE BACKGROUND, ALONG WITH A VARIETY OF BACTERIA.

The ANATOMY of Poop

So what *exactly* is poop made of, and why does it smell so bad? Let's take a super-close look and find out.

A typical human bowel movement is about 75 percent water (even if it seems pretty solid). This makes feces soft and squishy enough to get squeezed along through the intestines. However, poop also contains a lot of other equally important ingredients.

75% water

The other 25%:

Bilirubin
This chemical is made of broken-down dead red blood cells, and it gives poop its brown color.

Dead human cells
Cells from your intestines and other parts of the digestive system that have died and been replaced also need to exit your body.

Mucus coating
Feces also has a covering of slimy mucus (similar to snot) to make it slippery, helping it to make a smooth exit.

Old food
Foods your body can't digest easily include fruit cores and grain husks. This old food starts to break down in the guts, so it comes out as a mushy sludge.

Bacteria and yeast
One bowel movement can contain more than a trillion bacteria and yeast cells. These single-celled creatures live in your intestine and help to break down and digest food. As they keep reproducing and growing, loads of them leave your body with each trip to the bathroom.

Other substances, such as fats, proteins, and minerals

It's a STINKY ONE!

As the bacteria in your stomach digest and break down food, they release several gases and other smelly chemicals that cause poop to stink. Many of them contain sulfur, the bad-smelling mineral that also wafts from volcanoes and rotten eggs. Scientists think we've evolved to find the smell extra gross, as some of the germs in poop can be harmful and spread diseases. Finding it revolting makes sure we avoid it, helping us to stay safer.

POOP PERFECTION

WANT TO KNOW IF YOUR POOP PASSES MUSTER? ACCORDING TO DOCTORS, A PERFECTLY FORMED AND HEALTHY POO SHOULD TICK ALL THESE BOXES:

💩 ONE CONTINUOUS PIECE (OR TWO AT MOST)
💩 SOFT AND EASY TO GET OUT
💩 MEDIUM TO DARK BROWN
💩 ABOUT THE DIAMETER OF THE CIRCLE YOU CAN MAKE WITH YOUR FINGER AND THUMB
💩 SHOULD SINK, NOT FLOAT

FUNKY SKUNKS!

THINK OF A TERRIBLE-SMELLING ANIMAL AND A SKUNK IS SURE TO SPRING TO MIND. This furry, cat-size, black-and-white mammal carries the ultimate stink weapon: a yellow, oily, and unbelievably smelly liquid, which it can squirt straight at you from its rear end. Unless you want to end up drenched in one of the worst stenches in the world, never annoy a skunk!

STINKY BUT SWEET

Thanks to the risk of being squirted, many people are scared of skunks. But skunks are actually mild-mannered, gentle animals. They can even be helpful, as they feed on vermin and garbage, and can help keep farms and yards clean and tidy.

The problems only start when a skunk is cornered and frightened—especially if it has baby skunks to protect. If a predator or pet dog won't leave it alone, the skunk will end up with no choice but to defend itself and its family by spraying. And the way that happens really is disgusting ...

THIS SKUNK IS SCARED AND ABOUT TO SPRAY ... STAND BACK!

GROSS GLANDS

A skunk sprays using two small organs found on either side of its rear. Many mammals have these glands, but a skunk's are extra-well-developed and large. When the skunk is about to spray, two small nozzles emerge from the glands, which the skunk can actually use to take aim at its enemy. Then it squeezes hard, and a stream of gloopy yellow gunk comes squirting out. The skunk can accurately aim the spray where it wants to, up to about eight feet (2.4 m) away. Or, if it's dark and the skunk can't see its target clearly, it will spray the smelly liquid in a cloudy mist instead, to make sure the predator can't avoid it.

GLANDS

SPRAY

cooking gas
sewers
rotten onions   rotten eggs
burning rubber
ammonia   decaying meat
cat pee   old sweat
poop
rotten cabbage

A SICKENING STINK

People who have smelled skunk spray up close say there's no simple way to describe it. It's so strong that it makes your eyes water, and it even makes some people throw up. It's made of powerful chemicals called thiols, which contain the stinky mineral sulfur (also found in rotten eggs, raw onions, and volcanic gases). See the image to the left to find out how people describe the stench! If you could simply wash yourself or your dog off in the shower, it wouldn't be so bad. But the smell of skunk spray is notoriously hard to get rid of. According to folk remedies, washing in tomato juice is supposed to work. But there are many tales of clothes, cars, garages, and even homes that have never stopped smelling of skunk after an unlucky spraying incident.

MANY ANIMALS USE GLANDS IN THEIR REAR TO MARK THEIR TERRITORY WITH SCENT. THE LIQUID IS STRONG SMELLING AND LONG LASTING, SO THAT OTHER ANIMALS WILL STILL BE ABLE TO SMELL IT DAYS LATER.

CUTE BABY SKUNKS

DON'T GET SPRAYED!

FOLLOW THESE SIMPLE TIPS TO MAKE SURE YOU DON'T BECOME SKUNK TARGET PRACTICE.

🐾 **AVOID SKUNKS**
IF YOU SEE A SKUNK, GIVE IT A WIDE BERTH.

🐾 **REMEMBER BREEDING SEASON**
SKUNKS USUALLY HAVE THEIR BABIES, CALLED KITS, IN FEBRUARY AND MARCH. AT THIS TIME OF YEAR, BE EXTRA CAREFUL NOT TO GET TOO CLOSE TO EASILY ALARMED SKUNK PARENTS.

🐾 **KEEP YOUR COOL**
DON'T SCREAM, YELL, RUN AROUND IN CIRCLES, OR WAVE YOUR ARMS IN A PANIC—YOU'LL MAKE THINGS WORSE! JUST KEEP CALM AND STEP AWAY FROM THE SKUNK.

🐾 **WATCH OUT FOR WARNING SIGNS**
A WORRIED SKUNK WILL WARN YOU IT'S ABOUT TO SPRAY BY STAMPING ITS FEET, GROWLING, ARCHING ITS BACK, AND LIFTING ITS TAIL. SOME TYPES, LIKE THE SPOTTED SKUNK, MAY DO A HANDSTAND. IF THIS HAPPENS, BACK AWAY SLOWLY!

🐾 **DUCK!**
IF IT'S TOO LATE AND THE SKUNK DOES SPRAY YOU, TRY TO DUCK OR JUMP OUT OF THE WAY AT THE LAST SECOND. IT COULD SAVE YOUR SKIN!

REVOLTING RECORDS

WE'VE ALL HEARD OF RECORD-BREAKING RUNNING, CHAMPION CUP STACKING, AND OTHER FABULOUS FEATS, SUCH AS CREATING THE WORLD'S TALLEST SANDCASTLE OR BIGGEST PIZZA.

But did you know that there are a whole bunch of lesser known, but much more revolting, world records that lots of people compete over? Read on to find out which records take the cake for world's grossest.

YUCK-O-METER
EWW · GROSS · NASTY · DISGUSTING

Eye Milk SQUIRTING

> **RECORD TO BEAT:** 9.2 feet (2.8 m)

Never mind being world champion. It's gross enough to suck milk up your nose and squirt it out of your eye in the first place! Not everyone can do this. But a small number of people can, because the insides of their noses have an unusual shape and are connected to their eyes. With practice, they can learn to squirt liquids held inside their nose out of the corner of their eye and into the air.

In 2004, a Turkish man named Ilker Yilmaz secured the record by squirting milk a total of 9.2 feet (2.8 m) from his eye into a cup at the other end of the table! It's probably safe to say that no one saved the milk afterward to use in their coffee.

> YILMAZ FIRST REALIZED HE COULD SQUIRT LIQUID OUT OF HIS EYE WHEN HE WAS IN A SWIMMING POOL!

ILKER YILMAZ DEMONSTRATES HIS EYE-SQUIRTING SKILLS.

CREEPY COLLECTIONS

YOU DON'T HAVE TO DO SOMETHING GROSS TO CLAIM A REVOLTING WORLD RECORD ... YOU COULD JUST *COLLECT* SOMETHING GROSS INSTEAD. CHECK OUT THESE REPULSIVE RECORD-BREAKING COLLECTIONS OF BARF-INDUCING BODY BITS.

BELLY BUTTON LINT
AUSTRALIAN LIBRARIAN GRAHAM BARKER BEGAN COLLECTING THE FLUFF FROM HIS BELLY BUTTON IN 1984 ... AND NEVER STOPPED! BY 2010, HE WAS ABLE TO BAG HIMSELF A WORLD RECORD, WITH THREE FULL JARS OF LINT, WEIGHING A TOTAL OF 22.1 GRAMS, OR 0.8 OUNCE.

TOENAIL CLIPPINGS
STRANGE AS IT MAY SEEM, THERE ARE QUITE A FEW PEOPLE WHO DON'T THROW THEIR TOENAIL CLIPPINGS AWAY AND SAVE THEM IN A BOX OR JAR INSTEAD. OVER TIME, THEY'VE BUILT UP HUGE HEAPS OF CLIPPINGS, WITH SEVERAL CONTENDERS CLAIMING TO HAVE THE MOST. HOWEVER, THE WORLD RECORD GOES TO A BUNCH OF CANADIAN SCIENTISTS, WHO COLLECTED 24,999 PEOPLE'S TOENAIL CLIPPINGS FOR A HEALTH STUDY IN 2013.

Moving Maggots BY MOUTH

> RECORD TO BEAT: 37 pounds (16.8 kg) of maggots in one hour

Why would you want to use your mouth to move large numbers of live, wriggly maggots from one place to another? No one knows! But this is an official world record, set in 2009 by British "Maggot Man" Charlie Bell. He had to repeatedly slurp the maggots from a large container into his mouth, carry them over to another container, and spit them out—as fast as possible. To make matters worse, some of the maggots started to hatch out into adult flies! Afterward, Bell said he'd almost had to stop because the maggots smelled so bad, and, unsurprisingly, he described his ordeal as "disgusting."

PEOPLE WHO KEEP PILES OF TOENAIL CLIPPINGS HAVE TO KEEP THEIR PRIZED COLLECTION CLEAN AND CAREFULLY BAGGED UP. OTHERWISE, TINY BUGS START TO FEED ON THEM, AND THE COLLECTION SHRINKS.

SNAILS on Face

> RECORD TO BEAT: 48

If you're not so great at pole-vaulting or sailing around the world, an easier way to win a world record might be to put a lot of snails on your face. This record has been broken and rebroken several times, from early records of just 8, then 15, and finally up to almost 50 snails when Australian Mike Dalton set a new 48-snail record in 2009.

For a successful attempt, the challenger must have as many snails as possible put on their face within one minute. Judges then count the number of snails that stay on for at least another 10 seconds. Though that doesn't sound like long, it's not easy. Past competitors describe the snails as slimy, cold, and "tingly" as they gently nibble at your skin. Yuck!

A COMPETITOR LETS SNAILS CRAWL ON HER FACE.

WHAT'S LIVING ON YOU?

DID YOU KNOW YOUR BODY IS NOT JUST A NICE, COZY HOME FOR YOU, BUT FOR LOTS OF OTHER ITSY-BITSY LIVING THINGS TOO? And we're not just talking a few creatures here and there—there are billions of them, swarming over your skin, hair, and eyelashes at all times. Some are even inside you. Some you might be able to spot, while others are too small to see. Read on to get a microscopic view of the creepy critters that call you home.

SKIN BACTERIA KEEP MULTIPLYING AND MAKING MORE BACTERIA. AT THE SAME TIME, YOU KEEP SHEDDING OLD, DEAD SKIN CELLS, AND BACTERIA FALL OFF ALONG WITH THEM.

COVERED IN CRITTERS

Take a look at the palm of your hand. You can't see them, but there are actually thousands of single-celled bacteria and fungi living there—as well as all over the rest of you. They feed on dead skin cells, other bacteria, sweat, or oils made by skin. They especially like to hang out on your face, in between fingers and toes, and in your armpits!

But wait—don't rush to scrub them all off! It's normal and healthy to be covered in microscopic creepy-crawlies from head to toe. Really! Many of these microbes are harmless, and some actually help you by fighting off more dangerous germs that you pick up from your surroundings.

It *is* important to wash your hands, of course, especially after touching something that could harbor harmful germs, such as a toilet or raw meat. And when bacteria feed on sweat, they make waste chemicals that start to stink after a day or two. Yep—the stink of unwashed feet and armpits is basically the smell of bacteria poop! So it makes sense to practice good hygiene to keep smelling fresh.

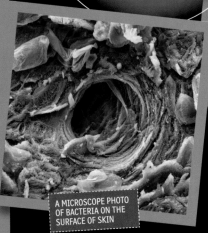

A MICROSCOPE PHOTO OF BACTERIA ON THE SURFACE OF SKIN

EYELASH MITES BURROW INTO HAIR FOLLICLES TO FEED ON SEBUM, A NATURAL OILY SUBSTANCE MADE IN THE SKIN.

MILLIONS OF MITES

Do you hate spiders? Would you prefer that they weren't walking around on your face? We hate to tell you, but there's a good chance you have little creepy-crawly, spiderlike creatures called eyelash mites living in your eyelashes and eyebrows. In fact, most of us do! Mites are a type of tiny eight-legged animal, though you still need a microscope to see them. They live in and around the hair follicles—the tiny openings in the skin that your eyelashes and eyebrow hairs grow out of.

You pick up eyelash mites from other people. The older you are, and the more people you've hung out with, the more likely you are to have them. But don't panic! They're a normal feature of your body, and most people never notice them.

UNINVITED GUESTS

BESIDES THE CREATURES THAT LIVE IN OR ON YOU FULL-TIME, YOU MAY SOMETIMES HAVE UNWELCOME INVADERS. HEAD LICE, A TYPE OF INSECT, MAY CRAWL OVER FROM OTHER PEOPLE'S HEADS TO SET UP HOME IN YOUR HAIR. THEY CAN CAUSE TROUBLE, AS THEY SUCK YOUR BLOOD AND MAKE YOUR HEAD ITCH, AS WELL AS LAYING STICKY EGGS CALLED NITS. LUCKILY, YOU CAN BANISH THEM USING SPECIAL HAIR OIL AND COMBING THE LICE AND NITS OUT—THOUGH IT'S NOT MUCH FUN!

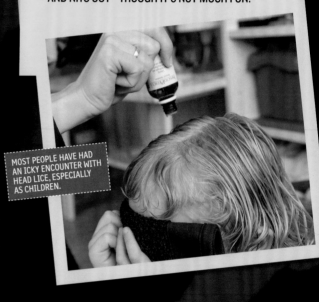

MOST PEOPLE HAVE HAD AN ICKY ENCOUNTER WITH HEAD LICE, ESPECIALLY AS CHILDREN.

JUST A FEW OF THE HUNDREDS OF SPECIES OF BACTERIA IN A HUMAN GUT

BACTERIA BONANZA

Your skin may be home to a lot of bacteria, but it's far from the busiest place in your body. The ultimate microbe metropolis is in your large intestine, where waste is formed. Around 40 *trillion* bacteria are crowded in there—around the same as the total number of cells in the human body itself! The bacteria take up less space than the rest of your body, though, as they're a lot smaller than the average body cell. That's just as well, or you'd be lugging the equivalent of another whole human around!

Like skin microbes, these tiny gut tenants are mostly helpful, not harmful. They help you digest food, and they keep your intestines working well. Scientists think they may control other things as well, such as how stressed you feel. So "gut feelings" like worry and fear may really be linked to those critters in your gut!

CREEPY-CRAWLIES HAVE SOMETIMES BEEN FOUND LIVING INSIDE PEOPLE'S EARS. THEY'VE INCLUDED A CRICKET, A SPIDER, A MOTH, AND A BEDBUG (NOT ALL TOGETHER, THOUGH)!

HORRIBLE HABITS OF ANCIENT ROME

YUCK-O-METER

EWW · GROSS · NASTY · DISGUSTING

THE ANCIENT ROMANS ARE FAMOUS FOR THEIR ENORMOUS EMPIRE AND CIVILIZED CULTURE. They built roads, theaters, and swimming pools that still stand today. They had complex political and military systems and fancy dinner parties. But they also had some putrid personal habits that will make you go *eww!*

Please Pass the SPONGE

The Romans had communal public toilets with a channel underneath to carry away their waste (see page 11). However, they didn't have toilet paper. For wiping, each public toilet had a natural sea sponge affixed to a stick, called a xylospongium. Only, it wasn't meant for one person—the sponge was passed around and shared by everyone. It was also used to scrub down the toilets!

In fact, Roman toilets were not very clean in general. They may have been well designed and built to last, but they were full of creepy-crawly lice, germs, and rats. Even worse, they sometimes exploded! Methane gas from the rotting poop would collect in the underground sewer pipes. If someone went too close with a flame, such as an oil lamp, *BOOM!*

ROMANS ENJOY A MID-POOP CHAT.

THESE TOGAS LOOK CLEAN, BUT THEY MAY HAVE SMELLED TERRIBLE.

INSTEAD OF WASHING THEIR BODIES WITH SOAP, THE ROMANS RUBBED THEMSELVES WITH OIL, THEN SCRAPED OFF THE GRIME AND DEAD SKIN USING A TOOL CALLED A STRIGIL.

The Not-so-Dry CLEANERS

"Ugh, what's that smell?" "Oh, it's my toga. I just got it back from the cleaners!"

OK, ancient Romans probably didn't have this exact conversation. But they probably did have smelly togas, as one of the main things the Romans used for washing their clothes was urine, or pee. Workers called *fullones* would collect the public's pee from vats left in the streets, or from people's homes, and take it to the laundries (or *fullonicae*). There, laundry slaves put the clothes in a urine bath and stomped on them to get them clean. Though it was gross, it did actually work. Pee contains a chemical called ammonia, which dissolves grease and bleaches out stains.

But it doesn't stop there. Ancient Roman writings also describe people using pee as a mouthwash to whiten their teeth! Urine was also a handy medicine and was dabbed onto burns, scrapes, and scorpion stings. And again, apart from the pungent odor, this wasn't such a bad idea, as ammonia can kill germs. (But don't try this at home—today we have cleaning and first aid methods that are much more sanitary.)

GLADIATOR Gore

All right, this one is really gross. Gladiators were trained fighters who were sent into armed combat against each other or dangerous wild animals as public entertainment in Roman times. It was normal for one or more gladiators in a show to end up dead. When this happened, the body was removed, and the gladiator's blood was collected, as the Romans believed it was a cure for a brain disease called epilepsy. You could buy some of the fresh gladiator blood, and—*gulp*—drink it as a medicine. Even more gruesome, some people thought that a gladiator's liver, a large body organ, was the best cure, so they ate that instead!

WILL ONE OF THESE UNFORTUNATE FIGHTERS END UP "DONATING" BODY PARTS FOR MEDICAL TREATMENTS?

THE VOMITORIUM: FACT OR FICTION?

A VOMITORIUM SOUNDS PRETTY DISGUSTING, DOESN'T IT? YOU MAY HAVE HEARD THAT THE ROMANS USED TO BARF INTO A SPECIAL TROUGH, OR VOMITORIUM, TO EMPTY THEIR STOMACHS SO THAT THEY COULD KEEP ON EATING A MASSIVE BANQUET. HOWEVER, THIS IS SOMETHING OF A ROMAN MYTH.

"VOMITORIUM" WAS ACTUALLY A WORD FOR THE PASSAGEWAYS LEADING OUT OF THEATERS AND SPORTS ARENAS, USED BECAUSE OF THE WAY PEOPLE POURED OUT OF THEM AFTER THE SHOW. HISTORIANS DON'T THINK THE ROMANS ACTUALLY LIKED TO PUKE UP DELIBERATELY BETWEEN COURSES.

QUIZ

HOW SQUEAMISH ARE YOU?

THE WORD "SQUEAMISH" DESCRIBES A PERSON WHO IS SENSITIVE TO ANYTHING DISGUSTING, SUCH AS STEPPING IN DOG POOP ON THE STREET, GETTING A WHIFF OF ROTTEN FOOD, OR SEEING A SQUASHED SLUG. **Curious about your own ability to withstand grossness? Take this quease-tastic quiz to find out where you score on the squeamishness scale!**

START HERE

YOU HAVE A LARGE SCAB. WHAT DO YOU DO WITH IT?

COVER IT WITH BANDAGES AND TRY NOT TO FAINT →

LEAVE IT ALONE AND FORGET ABOUT IT

PICK OR POKE AT IT, EVEN THOUGH YOU KNOW YOU SHOULDN'T

NO, OF COURSE NOT! EWWW!

HAVE YOU EVER EATEN A BOOGER?

GUINEA PIG

WHICH OF THESE WOULD YOU PREFER AS A PET?

LABRADOR →

UMMM … MAYBE?

BOA CONSTRICTOR

STOMACH OF STEEL

Nothing grosses you out. NO-THING. In fact, we have a sneaking suspicion you actually *like* all this gross stuff! And that's A-OK, because someone in this world has to perform gory surgeries and catch hairy spiders without batting an eyelid. But don't forget that things like puke and snot can be health hazards. Just make sure you wash your hands!

CALM IN A (GROSS) CRISIS

You're a handy person to have around when the snot hits the fan. When a gross or gruesome challenge rears its ugly head, you do what has to be done, even if you're gagging inside. Thank goodness someone around here is so sensible! Still, you're only human. There are some disgusting scenarios that even you can't cope with!

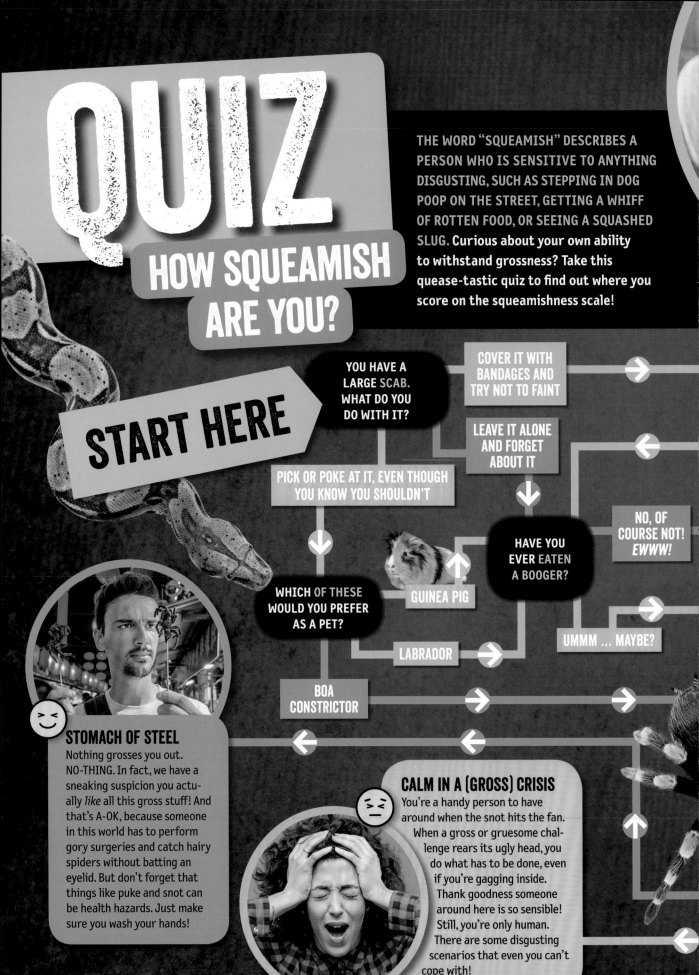

32

YOU OPEN A CARTON OF YOGURT TO FIND IT'S MOLDY. YOU ...

THROW IT IN THE TRASH AND GET ANOTHER

RUN AWAY! (TO GET HELP, OF COURSE)

SCREAM, FLING IT ACROSS THE ROOM, AND NEVER EAT YOGURT AGAIN

YOUR FRIEND FEELS SICK AND IS ABOUT TO THROW UP. YOU ...

HOLD OUT A BAG TO CATCH THE PUKE

STUDY IT UNDER A MAGNIFYING GLASS

HOW DO YOU DEAL WITH FINDING A SLUG IN THE KITCHEN?

KINDERGARTEN TEACHER

CALL THE POLICE

WHICH CAREER APPEALS TO YOU MORE?

CATCH IT WITH YOUR HANDS AND GIVE IT A NAME

CATCH IT IN A CUP AND PUT IT OUTSIDE

BRAIN SURGEON

WOULD YOU LIKE TO TRY A FRESHLY ROASTED TARANTULA?

YOU KNOW YOUR BODY IS HOME TO MILLIONS OF BACTERIA, RIGHT?

MAYBE IF YOU PAID ME A LOT

SURE, BUT THEY'RE MOSTLY HARMLESS

LA LA LA LAAA, I CAN'T HEAR YOU!

MMMM, SOUNDS CRUNCHY ... WHY NOT?

HOW DID YOU LIKE YOUR TARANTULA?

IT WAS OK, BUT I'LL ADD KETCHUP NEXT TIME!

I COULDN'T FINISH THE SLIMY BITS

SUPER SQUEAMISH!

Congratulations—you are the reigning champ of squeamishness! You scored so high on the squeam-o-meter, even everyday life kinda grosses you out. And when faced with blood, boogers, or writhing maggots, your screams can be heard from space. There's just one question—what on Earth are you doing reading this book?

PUTRID PROFESSIONS

GROSS NASTY
EWW DISGUSTING
YUCK-O-METER

WHAT DO YOU WANT TO DO WHEN YOU GROW UP? Whatever it is, you probably haven't considered one of these disgusting, smelly, or gruesome jobs! Luckily, many of them no longer exist, but a few do. In fact, some of them are really important …

IMAGINE HELPING HENRY VIII GO TO THE BATHROOM WHILE HE WAS WEARING ALL THIS!

GROOM OF THE STOOL

A Groom of the Stool was a royal servant in England, during the Tudor period of the 1400s and 1500s, who had the vital role of helping the king use the toilet, or "close-stool." This was a chair with a hole in it, with a bowl underneath to catch the king's waste. The Groom of the Stool had to keep the close-stool clean and fresh, have cloths and warm water ready for the king to use to clean himself, and assist him if needed. As the monarch wore heavy, luxurious clothes, the job also involved helping him to undress.

While waiting for the king to do his business, the Groom of the Stool was required to make polite conversation or to listen to the king gripe about work. This actually meant that Grooms of the Stool were often trusted advisors to monarchs, and some even became quite powerful in the royal court. So the job had its benefits!

KINGS APPOINTED A MAN AS GROOM OF THE STOOL. BUT IF THE MONARCH WAS FEMALE, LIKE QUEEN ELIZABETH I, THE JOB WENT TO A WOMAN AND WAS RENAMED "LADY OF THE BEDCHAMBER."

LEECH GATHERER

Leeches are wormlike animals that usually live in water. They either hunt smaller creepy-crawlies, or they latch their mouths on to larger animals, including humans, to suck their blood.

Long ago, leeches were used for bloodletting (removing blood from the body; see page 20), back when this was seen as a cure for various illnesses. In the 1800s, leech treatment really took off and became a huge craze in both Europe and North America. Hospitals needed a lot of leeches, and someone had to provide them. Enter the leech gatherer, whose job was to wander around in the swamps where leeches like to hang out, collecting as many as they could.

How did they collect them? Well, that's the really gross part. In muddy swamp water, it's hard to find a small, black leech just by looking. Instead, the leech gatherer would stand in the swamp in bare feet, until lots of hungry leeches had attached themselves to his or her legs. After a while, they picked them off and then started over. Not surprisingly, leech gatherers were often sick from loss of blood or from germs infecting their leech bites.

LEECHES CAN BE TINY, LIKE THIS ONE IN SUMATRA, INDONESIA, OR HUGE—SOME GROW UP TO 18 INCHES (46 CM) LONG.

POOP COLLECTOR

Throughout most of history, people didn't have flushing toilets and sewers. Wherever poop landed, there it would stay. This was a big problem in cities, where there were lots of people (and therefore lots of poop). So in many places around the world, workers called "night soil collectors," or sometimes "gong farmers," collected the feces. They would fill carts with poop and take it out of the city, where it could be dumped far away from human homes or used to make compost for farms. In fact, this still happens in some parts of the world.

ALL IN THE NAME OF SCIENCE

WE FIND THINGS LIKE POOP AND BACTERIA GROSS, PARTLY BECAUSE THEY CAN SPREAD DISEASES. BUT THAT ALSO MEANS SCIENTISTS NEED TO STUDY THEM TO LEARN MORE ABOUT HOW DISEASES WORK.

- A POOP ANALYST CAREFULLY EXAMINES POOP COLLECTED FROM PATIENTS TO CHECK FOR PROBLEMS. THE ANALYST LOOKS AT THE POOP UNDER A MICROSCOPE, CHECKS ITS COLOR AND TEXTURE, AND BREEDS BACTERIA FROM IT TO SEE WHAT THEY ARE. THIS CAN ALSO IDENTIFY DEADLY DISEASES AND HELP SAVE SOMEONE'S LIFE.

- AUSTRALIAN SCIENTISTS BARRY MARSHALL AND ROBIN WARREN FIGURED OUT THAT STOMACH ULCERS, WHICH CAN BE FATAL, WERE PROBABLY CAUSED BY A TYPE OF BACTERIA, *HELICOBACTER PYLORI.* BUT OTHER SCIENTISTS DIDN'T BELIEVE THEM. SO MARSHALL PREPARED A PETRI DISH FULL OF THE GERMS, TAKEN FROM A SICK PATIENT, AND DRANK IT! WITHIN DAYS HE BEGAN TO GET THE FIRST SYMPTOMS OF A STOMACH ULCER. THE PAIR THEN CURED IT WITH ANTIBIOTICS! AFTER BEING PROVEN RIGHT, MARSHALL AND WARREN WON THE NOBEL PRIZE FOR MEDICINE.

IN ANCIENT JAPAN, POOP FROM THE CITY WAS SOLD TO FARMERS AS A FERTILIZER. RICH PEOPLE'S POOP WAS CONSIDERED MORE VALUABLE BECAUSE THEY ATE FANCIER FOOD!

FOUL-SMELLING FEASTS

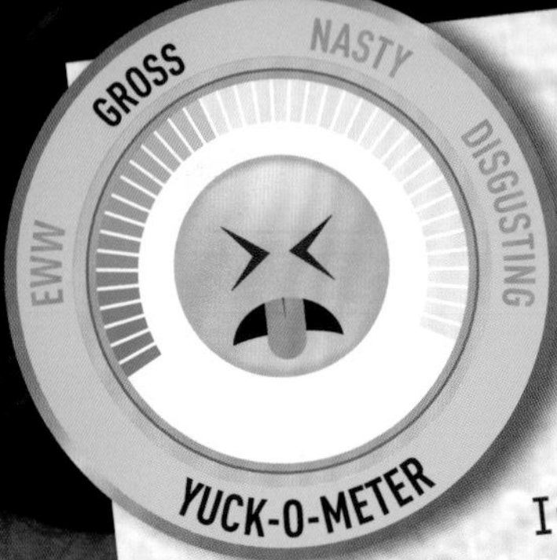

YOU NORMALLY USE YOUR NOSE TO HELP YOU DECIDE IF FOOD IS SAFE TO EAT OR NOT. If something from your refrigerator smells like cow dung, a dirty diaper, or six-day-old sweaty socks, that's usually a sign that you should *not* have it for lunch. Strangely, though, there are some foods that smell absolutely terrible but are still very popular. (Well, maybe not with everyone!) Could you bring yourself to try these super-stinky snacks?

CHEESY CHAMPION

In 2004, a panel of testers assembled at Cranfield University in England with an electronic smell-detecting machine to sniff out the world's whiffiest cheese. After two hours of inhaling cheesy aromas, they declared a winner: soft, creamy Vieux Boulogne from France.

So what does it smell like? Descriptions range from rotting vegetables, goats, and old earwax to cow dung, soil, dead leaves, and "eau de farmyard." Many types of cheese are quite stinky, but Vieux Boulogne is considered the worst.

TEMPTED? ALTHOUGH ITS SCENT IS STRONG, VIEUX BOULOGNE HAS A MILD TASTE—SO JUST HOLD YOUR NOSE AND YOU'LL BE FINE!

TIN CAN OF TERROR

Even the world's stinkiest cheese isn't as stinky as the Swedish delicacy called *surströmming* (pronounced soor-STRUMM-ing). It's a type of fermented fish that comes in a can, and it is a contender for the worst-smelling food in the world.

The fermenting process continues even after the fish is canned, so the cans start to bulge and swell with the putrid gases inside. The smell when the can is first opened is so horrific that Sweden's government actually issues advice on how to handle it. First, you have to go outdoors to open the can, or the smell will stink up your home. Some people put the can inside a plastic bag to catch any smelly juice splats. Others swear by opening the can underwater. Either way, it releases a reek that resembles a mixture of used diapers, rotten eggs, rancid butter, vinegar, and dog poop!

Once it's opened, and you've recovered from the smell, the official advice is to go back indoors—otherwise your disgusting delicacy will attract too many flies! Yuck. Like many stinky foods, though, it doesn't taste quite as awful as it smells. The taste is usually described as fishy, strong, and salty. Many Swedes love it in a sandwich with potatoes and sour cream.

THE DURIAN IS GREEN, SPIKY, AND UP TO A FOOT (30.5 CM) LONG, WITH SOFT YELLOW FLESH INSIDE.

THE ENDURING ODOR OF DURIAN

This famously foul-smelling food from Southeast Asia isn't cheesy or fishy, and it isn't fermented or rotted in any way. It's just a large, green, fresh fruit from the forest. Yet its stench is so powerful that it lingers for days after someone has eaten one, and it can be smelled from yards away. Eating, or even carrying, a durian is banned in many of Southeast Asia's hotels, buses, and trains. So what is the smell like? There have been many attempts to pin it down in words, with comparisons including:

- ✕ Smelly socks
- ✕ Pig poop
- ✕ Turpentine
- ✕ Rotten onions
- ✕ Toilets
- ✕ Dead rats
- ✕ Sewage
- ✕ Burnt rubber

WHAT YOUR NOSE KNOWS

HOW CAN SOMETHING SMELL REPULSIVE BUT TASTE OK? WELL, THE LINKS BETWEEN TASTE AND SMELL CAN BE COMPLICATED. WHEN YOU SMELL SOMETHING, YOU USE A SET OF SCENT-DETECTING CELLS INSIDE THE TOP OF YOUR NOSE, CLOSE TO YOUR BRAIN. WHEN YOU TASTE, YOU USE THE TASTE BUDS ON YOUR TONGUE AND AROUND YOUR MOUTH, AND YOUR SENSE OF SMELL AS WELL, AS THE SCENT OF THE FOOD WAFTS UP YOUR NOSE FROM YOUR MOUTH.

TASTE BUDS CAN DETECT ONLY A FEW SIMPLE TASTES: SALTY, SWEET, BITTER, SOUR, AND UMAMI (SAVORY). BUT IF THE FOOD TASTES STRONGLY OF ONE OF THESE, LIKE SWEET DURIAN OR SALTY SURSTRÖMMING, YOU DON'T NOTICE THE SMELL PART AS MUCH.

FOODS DON'T ALWAYS TASTE THE SAME AS THEY SMELL.

PREDATORY PLANTS

IMAGINE WANDERING IN A RAINFOREST WHEN YOU ACCIDENTALLY STEP ON SOMETHING SMOOTH AND SLIMY. Splash! You slip headlong into a pool of gloopy liquid at the bottom of a deep pit. The sides are so slippery, you can't climb out. You've been trapped by a deadly pitcher plant, and now it's starting to digest you and swallow you up! OK—this couldn't actually happen to a human being. But if you were a beetle, a mouse, or a small lizard, it could. Some types of plants really do eat animals to help them get the nutrients they need. We're just lucky that those plants are on the small side—at least, those we've discovered so far!

FROG SOUP

PITCHER PLANTS ARE AMONG THE MOST FAMOUS CARNIVOROUS (OR MEAT-EATING) PLANTS. Some of their leaves form deep pitcherlike containers that collect rainwater. The plant adds its own slimy juices full of chemicals that can dissolve and digest meat. The slippery rim of each pitcher is covered in nectar, attracting insects and other small animals. Then, when the unsuspecting prey steps on the edge, it tumbles inside and drowns—or remains stuck until it is gradually dissolved. Once the prey is in liquid form, the plant can soak it up like a delicious bowl of soup.

A pitcher plant's regular diet is mostly made up of bugs such as flies, centipedes, and spiders. But the largest types sometimes catch frogs and lizards, and even whole rats!

THIS FROG NARROWLY ESCAPED BECOMING LUNCH.

THE BIGGEST PITCHER PLANT PITCHERS CAN REACH 16 INCHES (40 CM) LONG—AS BIG AS A WATERMELON.

A VENUS FLYTRAP SNAGS ITSELF A MEAL. SLURP!

NO ONE (SO FAR!) HAS EVER DISCOVERED A PLANT THAT COULD EAT A WHOLE HUMAN. EVEN IF YOU PUT YOUR FINGER IN A PITCHER PLANT OR VENUS FLYTRAP, THE DIGESTION PROCESS IS SO SLOW THAT IT WOULDN'T HURT YOU. SCIENTISTS HAVE FED BITS OF HUMAN SKIN TO VENUS FLYTRAPS, THOUGH, WHICH THEY HAPPILY GOBBLED UP.

HOWEVER, PLANTS THAT CAN EAT—AND EVEN CHASE AND CATCH—HUMANS DO EXIST IN FOLKTALES, BOOKS, AND PLAYS:

- IN THE SCI-FI NOVEL *THE DAY OF THE TRIFFIDS*, BY JOHN WYNDHAM, TRIFFIDS ARE SEVEN-FOOT (2.1-M)-TALL WALKING PLANTS THAT KILL PEOPLE BY LASHING AT THEM WITH A DEADLY POISONOUS TENDRIL—AND THEN SLURP UP THEIR BODIES.
- *LITTLE SHOP OF HORRORS* IS A FILM TURNED MUSICAL ABOUT A FLORIST WHO ACCIDENTALLY GROWS A MONSTER CARNIVOROUS PLANT. IT LEARNS TO SPEAK AND DEMANDS HUMAN FLESH!
- IN THE 1800S, SEVERAL REPORTS AND NEWS STORIES ABOUT AFRICA DESCRIBED HUMAN-EATING TREES WITH SNAKELIKE TENTACLES THAT COULD GRAB AND DEVOUR A WHOLE PERSON. ONE WAS CALLED THE *YA-TE-VEO*, MEANING "I SEE YOU." YIKES! BUT THESE TALES TURNED OUT TO BE TOTALLY MADE UP.

BEWARE OF PLANT!

PITCHER PLANTS ARE PRETTY DEADLY, BUT AT LEAST THEY DON'T BITE. A Venus flytrap does! Even though it's just a plant, it has a set of "jaws" made from specially shaped leaves—and they even have tooth-shaped parts along the edges. The flytrap allows its jaws to hang open, ready for some lunch to fly or crawl in. If an unwary insect sits on the inside of the leafy "mouth," then ... snap! The jaws snap closed, and the creepy "teeth" stop prey from escaping.

Once the victim is trapped, the plant checks if it really has caught something worth eating (and not just a dead leaf, for example). It does this by waiting to see if the insect wriggles! If it does, this triggers hairs on the insides of the leaves. The "jaws" stick together to make a sealed pocket and then release the digestive juices to dissolve the prey.

WHY MUNCH MEAT?

IF IT SOUNDS WEIRD FOR A PLANT TO EAT MEAT, THAT'S BECAUSE IT IS! Only a few types of plants do it, including pitcher plants, flytraps, and sundews, which catch and digest flies using sticky globs of mucus on stalks. These plants grow in poor soil or bogs, which don't contain all the nutrients plants need to grow. Snapping up a few flies or frogs keeps them healthy!

A SUNDEW LEAF CURLS AROUND A TRAPPED LACEWING.

THE ART OF DISGUST

DON'T TRY THIS AT HOME!

NASTY
GROSS
EWW
DISGUSTING

YUCK-O-METER

IN THE AGE OF MODERN ART, (ALMOST) ANYTHING GOES—FROM SCULPTURES MADE OF PILES OF TRASH TO BLANK CANVASES WITH NOTHING PAINTED ON THEM. Art like this is often meant to make a statement, ask a question, or make you think. Sometimes it's designed to be as weird or shocking as possible.

So it's not really surprising that some artists and sculptors have decided to make art featuring some decidedly disgusting, gross, or spooky ingredients like animal dung, bacteria, or even the artist's own blood! Read on to find out more about icky artistic ingredients you'll want to avoid.

FLYING FECES

What's that over there? It's an enormous pile of poop flying through the sky, of course! Yes, this actually happened. An airborne megapoop the size of a house was the work of American artist Paul McCarthy, who has created various incredibly realistic-looking poop models. In 2008, his giant inflatable poop sculpture was sitting on the grounds of an art gallery in Switzerland when strong winds broke the ropes tying it down and blew it away. It sailed more than 600 feet (182 m) and crashed into several buildings before landing in someone's garden. Oops! Or should that be … poops!

But why stop at fake poop? British artist Chris Ofili caused controversy in the 1990s when he created paintings and collages featuring glitter, glue, and lumps of real elephant dung. The dung wasn't stinky, as it had been specially treated to kill germs and stop smells, but plenty of people were still outraged. They obviously had no idea that art can get even grosser than that!

BEWARE OF LOW-FLYING POOP!

ONE OF MARC QUINN'S FROZEN BLOOD HEAD SCULPTURES, NAMED "SELF."

ONE OF QUINN'S "SELF" BLOOD HEADS CONTAINS THE SAME AMOUNT OF BLOOD AS THERE IS IN THE WHOLE OF AN AVERAGE HUMAN BODY.

CANNED CACA

Italian artist Piero Manzoni may have created the ultimate, and much more revolting, poop art many years earlier in 1961. He simply filled 90 small cans with his own waste, sealed them shut, and labeled them *Merda d'artista*—that is, Artist's Poop. He even set a price for them: Each can would be worth its weight in gold, which was about $37 at the time.

At least, Manzoni said they were full of his waste. Were they really? A friend of his has claimed he really just put plaster inside to give the cans a little weight. There are rumors that some of the cans have leaked or been opened, but it's not clear what was found.

Manzoni claimed he was making a mockery of the art market, and the fact that people would buy anything if they thought it was art. He was right! The cans sold for high prices. Britain's famous Tate Gallery has one, and another fetched a whopping (or plopping) price of over $323,000 at an auction in 2016.

BUST OF BLOOD

Making art from poop is seriously gross, but at least poop is easy to get ahold of. When British sculptor Marc Quinn decided to make a sculpture using his own blood, he had to collect it over a period of several years, since people can't lose too much blood at once. Then, Quinn made a cast of his own head, and used about 11 pints (5 L) of blood to fill it. The blood was frozen to make the finished head sculpture. And every five years, Quinn makes a new version of the blood head to keep track of the changes in his appearance.

ARMPIT ART

Korean artist Anicka Yi uses armpit sweat, body bacteria, germs, and bugs in her art—which is not just for looking at but also for smelling! She creates perfumes from chemicals collected from people's armpits, and she grows bacteria samples in dishes that are displayed in her exhibitions. The stinky scents are squirted around the gallery—and at visitors as they enter—to give guests a multisensory stinky art experience.

DARINGLY DISGUSTING DUCHAMP

SOME SAY MODERN ART ITSELF BEGAN WITH A GROSS-THEMED SCULPTURE THAT SHOCKED THE PUBLIC WAY BACK IN 1917. MARCEL DUCHAMP, A SCULPTOR AND PAINTER FROM FRANCE, SUBMITTED A SCULPTURE TO AN EXHIBITION IN NEW YORK. IT WAS A PORCELAIN URINAL FROM A MEN'S PUBLIC TOILET, TURNED ON ITS SIDE, WITH THE STRANGE SIGNATURE "R. MUTT" WRITTEN ON IT. DUCHAMP NAMED IT "FOUNTAIN." THE EXHIBITION ORGANIZERS REFUSED TO ACCEPT IT, BUT A PHOTOGRAPHER, ALFRED STIEGLITZ, AGREED TO DISPLAY IT IN HIS STUDIO INSTEAD. THIS GAVE ARTISTS A NEW WAY OF THINKING. IF THEY WANTED TO TURN SOMETHING INTO ART, THEY COULD— WHATEVER IT MIGHT BE!

FAMOUS AMERICAN ARTIST ANDY WARHOL INVITED HIS FRIENDS TO PEE ON ART CANVASES THAT HE HAD TREATED WITH CHEMICALS. THE URINE REACTED WITH THE CHEMICALS TO MAKE PATTERNS!

R. MUTT 1917

SULTANS OF SLIME

YUCK-O-METER

EWW · GROSS · NASTY · DISGUSTING

WHAT'S THE MOST DISGUSTING CREATURE ON PLANET EARTH? There are several contenders, but many people would pick the body-burrowing, slime-creating, nightmarish-looking hagfish. These unbelievably awesome and somewhat revolting deep-sea fish are also nicknamed "slime eels" and "snot snakes." But they don't care—to them, slime is superb!

GRODY GLOOP

Hagfish are famous for their astonishing slimemaking abilities. When a hungry predator tries to grab a hagfish in its mouth, it will suddenly find the fish is covered in thick, gloopy, supremely sticky slime. It's hard for the hunter to hang on when it has a mouth full of slippery goop. If it's a shark or other fish, the slime can also clog its gills and stop it from breathing. The predator soon lets go of the hagfish—and learns to leave them alone!

Hagfish seem to produce a vast amount of slime, but how can one small fish make so much? The secret is that the hagfish don't actually squirt out all the slime. Instead, they release very thin, fine threads from holes along their sides—similar to the way a spider produces threads of spider silk. When the hagfish threads combine with water, they expand to make the stringy, stretchy, gel-like slime.

IN EXPERIMENTS, WHEN SCIENTISTS PUT A HAGFISH INTO A BUCKET OF WATER, ALL THE WATER IN THE BUCKET TURNED INTO SLIME WITHIN MINUTES.

READY FOR YOUR
CLOSE-UP, HAGFISH?

THE THIRD WEDNESDAY IN OCTOBER EVERY YEAR IS **HAGFISH DAY.** IT WAS CREATED TO CELEBRATE THE FACT THAT EVEN "UNATTRACTIVE" WILDLIFE CAN BE IMPORTANT AND USEFUL AND SHOULD NOT BE IGNORED.

A SLIPPERY ESCAPE

However, this doesn't mean the hagfish ends up choked and swamped by its own slime. The cunning critter has a brilliant way to escape. It gives a kind of snotty sneeze to expel the slime from its nostrils and ties a knot in its body. Then it runs the knot along the whole length of its body, wiping the slime off and also pushing off any predator that still has a hold on it. Genius!

BODY BURROWERS

But the grossness doesn't stop there. Hagfish are scavengers, feeding on the dead bodies of other sea creatures that sink down onto the seabed. The slimy fish has waggling tentacles around its mouth that it uses to smell and feel its way to food. Then the hagfish clamps its rows of horror-movie teeth on to the carcass, and it starts to chomp and munch its way inside the dead flesh face-first, making a tunnel as it goes. When it wants to back out of the hole it has made in the body, it uses the knot-tying trick to slide itself out.

FREAKY FACE

This is not a face you'd want to see before bed. The hagfish's repulsive reputation isn't helped by the fact that it looks like the grossest, most terrifying sci-fi monster you could imagine. Around the bottom half of its face are its sharp teeth, with two rows on each side of a wide, gaping mouth. Around the top are the wriggly food-finding tentacles. The hagfish looks even more alien because it doesn't really have any eyes—just small, basic "eye-spots" that can sense the difference between light and dark (but not much else). Sleep tight!

The hagfish's body is very flexible. While it has teeth and a skull, it doesn't have many other bones. Its pinkish gray skin isn't scaly, but smooth and slightly loose, kind of like a rumpled sock. Hagfish are usually around 20 inches (51 cm) long, but the biggest can grow to more than four feet (1.2 m).

SUPER SLIME

WHEN IT'S DRIED OUT, SCIENTISTS CAN EXTRACT THE SUPERFINE, THIN THREADS OF HAGFISH SLIME. EACH ONE IS ONLY ABOUT A HUNDREDTH OF THE THICKNESS OF A HUMAN HAIR. BECAUSE THE THREADS ARE STRONG AND FLEXIBLE, LIKE SPIDER SILK, SCIENTISTS THINK THEY COULD ONE DAY BE USED TO MAKE VERY LIGHT, TOUGH FABRICS FOR PARACHUTES OR BULLETPROOF VESTS.

HELPFUL HAGFISH

THOUGH THEY SEEM PRETTY DISGUSTING, HAGFISH DO AN IMPORTANT JOB IN THE OCEANS. LIKE OTHER SCAVENGERS, THEY DISPOSE OF OLD, DEAD BODIES, KEEPING THE ECOSYSTEM CLEAN.

GROSS GREEN BOOGERS

NASTY
GROSS
DISGUSTING
EWW
YUCK-O-METER

DO YOU EVER PICK YOUR NOSE? *Shh,* we won't tell. Hey, you're not doing it right now, are you? Well, if you are, you're not alone—almost everyone has picked their nose at some point. Many people even do it every day. However, they usually do it in private. Otherwise, people will get grossed out at seeing those crispy, gooey, or slimy boogers! Disgusting! But how bad are boogers, really?

YOUR NOSE MAKES OVER 4.8 CUPS (1.1 L) OF MUCUS EACH DAY! MOST OF IT ENDS UP IN YOUR STOMACH.

A BOOGER IS BORN

To find out where boogers come from, you have to know about mucus. Mucus is a slimy, sticky, gloopy substance made inside your nose and several other body parts.

Nose mucus is often called snot. It lines the inside of the nose and throat, making sure they don't dry out. Because it's sticky, mucus also catches germs, dirt, dust, pollen, and other bits and pieces in the air that you breathe in. This stops the debris from entering the lungs, where it could cause damage. Mucus can even kill some types of germs.

Once an unwanted item is caught, tiny hairs waft the mucus toward the nostrils to get rid of the stuck muck. On the way, the mucus starts to dry out, and it forms the lumps and nasty nuggets we know as boogers. Left to themselves, they'd eventually flake away and fall out of your nose bit by bit. But some people just can't resist digging them out first!

BURIED TREASURE

Why do people pick the boogers out of their noses? Sometimes, snot stuck in your nose feels uncomfortable or itchy, so you want it out. But humans also seem to have a natural compulsion to pick at things, whether it's a booger, a scab, a zit, or peeling wallpaper. It just feels satisfying when you bag that booger. *Ahhh!*

Bad news, though: Doctors warn that nose-picking isn't very good for you. Too much picking can damage the inside of your nose or even cause a nosebleed. And nose-picking can leave germs on your fingers, which are then spread around. To solve these problems, the best way to remove those boogies is by blowing them out politely, using a tissue.

SNOTTY SNACKS

As gross as it may seem, plenty of people really do eat the boogers they pick out. Some can't be bothered to find a tissue, or they don't want to get caught wiping the snot on a wall or under a desk. Some people like the taste! Picking your nose and eating it even has a scientific name: mucophagy.

Despite the horror you might feel at the thought of chowing down on a phlegmy feast, scientists say booger-munching isn't actually bad for you. In fact, most of the mucus your nose makes runs down the back of your throat and gets swallowed anyway. Eating a booger is no different—it's just a little more dried out, with an extra helping of dust and germs. Most of the germs die once they reach your stomach. Eating boogers may even improve your body's immune (or disease-fighting) system by helping it learn to recognize and kill different types of germs. Still, we'll pass on the mucus meal!

ACHOO! A MARINE IGUANA SNEEZES OUT A SALT BOOGER.

BEASTLY BOOGERS

- GIRAFFES CAN'T REACH THEIR NOSES WITH THEIR HOOVES, BUT THEY ARE STILL CHAMPION BOOGER-PICKERS. THEY USE THEIR LONG, THIN, RUBBERY TONGUES TO PICK THEIR NOSES!

- MARINE IGUANAS ARE AMONG THE WORLD'S SNEEZIEST ANIMALS. BECAUSE THEY SWIM IN THE SEA, THEIR BODIES COLLECT EXCESS SALT FROM THE SEAWATER. THEY SNEEZE THE SALT OUT OF THEIR NOSES, ALONG WITH RUNNY MUCUS.

- FOOTBALL-SIZE, GREEN, SLIMY "DRAGON BOOGERS" HAVE BEEN FOUND IN SOME LAKES AND RIVERS. SADLY, THEY'RE NOT REAL DRAGON BOOGERS—IT'S JUST A NAME FOR A TYPE OF SLIMY WATER CREATURE SIMILAR TO A JELLYFISH.

45

BLOODSUCKING BANDITS

NASTY
GROSS
EWW
DISGUSTING

YUCK-O-METER

YOUR BODY IS FULL OF BLOOD CONSTANTLY FLOWING THROUGH YOUR BLOOD VESSELS. Many of these vessels run close to your skin. And that means you're a great big living café for all kinds of small, bloodthirsty creatures who want to land on you and enjoy a yummy warm drink. Take a peek at our handy guide to help identify what's eating you!

WANTED!
FLEA

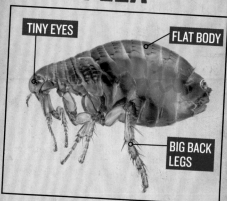

TINY EYES

FLAT BODY

BIG BACK LEGS

SLURP! A FLEA LOVES A MEAL OF HUMAN BLOOD.

DESCRIPTION: Tiny wingless insect that gets around by jumping on its big back legs

FOUND: Living on animals such as cats and dogs, and also on humans

APPEARANCE: 1/8 inch (0.3 cm) long; dark brown

MODE OF ATTACK: Hops onto you, sticks its sharp, needlelike mouthparts into your skin, and slurps up blood.

CRIMES: Leaves sore, itchy bites. Can spread terrible diseases, such as the bubonic plague (or Black Death).

ESCAPE ARTIST: Hard, flat body means it's very hard to squash! Leaps away from danger in the blink of an eye.

IN THE 1700S, PEOPLE OFTEN WORE FLEA TRAP NECKLACES. THEY CONTAINED BLOOD TO ATTRACT FLEAS, AND HONEY SO THEY WOULD GET STUCK!

WANTED!
TICK

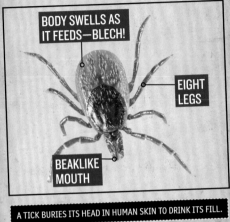

BODY SWELLS AS IT FEEDS—BLECH!

EIGHT LEGS

BEAKLIKE MOUTH

A TICK BURIES ITS HEAD IN HUMAN SKIN TO DRINK ITS FILL.

DESCRIPTION: Tiny spiderlike arthropod
FOUND: Worldwide, on animals and in vegetation
APPEARANCE: 1/8 inch (0.3 cm) long; yellow, brown, or black
MODE OF ATTACK: Waits on a plant stalk and grabs on to people and animals as they pass by. Cuts into skin using its saw-edged "beak," buries its head inside, and swells up as it feeds for days or weeks.
CRIMES: Spreads many diseases, including Lyme disease.
ESCAPE ARTIST: Has painkiller in its saliva, so victims don't notice they're being fed on.

WANTED!
BEDBUG

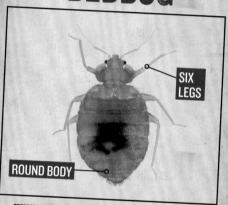

SIX LEGS

ROUND BODY

A BEDBUG SNEAKS A QUICK TASTE OF BLOOD AT NIGHT.

DESCRIPTION: Flat, round insect that looks like an apple seed
FOUND: In beds, furniture, and floorboards
APPEARANCE: 1/4 inch (0.6 cm) long; red-brown body
MODE OF ATTACK: Creeps out at night and pokes its long, sharp, strawlike mouth into human skin to suck blood.
CRIMES: Bites can cause an itchy rash or allergy.
ESCAPE ARTIST: If spotted in the night, it scuttles away and hides in bedding or cracks in furniture.

MOST WANTED!
MARAUDING MOSQUITO

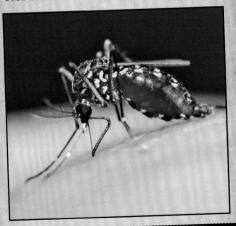

A MOSQUITO'S BODY FILLS UP WITH HUMAN BLOOD AS SHE FEEDS.

All these criminal creepy-crawlies can cause problems, but none of them are as dangerous as the mighty mosquito, found in warm, damp parts of the world. Like other bloodsuckers, they can pierce the skin with their sharp mouths and suck out blood. As they do so, germs carried in the mosquito's body can pass into the wound, spread into the host's blood, and sometimes cause disease. These diseases include West Nile virus, yellow fever, dengue fever, and—most dangerous of all—malaria. This often fatal infection is thought to have killed more people than any other disease in history—making mosquitoes the most wanted creepy-crawly killers of all time!

SLIPPERY, SLIMY SEWERS

YUCK-O-METER

EWW GROSS NASTY DISGUSTING

ARE YOU READY TO DESCEND INTO THE DISGUSTING DEPTHS THAT LIE BELOW OUR CITY STREETS? To visit or work in a sewer, you'll need a hazard suit, gloves, rubber boots, a harness (so you don't get swept away in a river of poop), an emergency oxygen supply, a hard hat, and a head-lamp. Get ready to find out just what puts the "ew" in "sewer"!

A PLACE FOR WASTE

Under the ground beneath your feet is a network of pipes and tunnels, some of them big enough to walk through. Waste from sinks, drains, and toilets flows into the sewer, where it is carried away to a sewage treatment plant to be sanitized. While some sewers are modern and made of metal, concrete, or plastic, many cities have huge sewer networks built from brick, sometimes hundreds of years old. Even ancient civilizations sometimes had sewers, like Babylonia, where clay sewer pipes were invented.

The normal way to get into a city's sewage system—unless you're a piece of poop, of course—is to climb down a manhole or utility hole. Most sewers are tunnels or tubes that run below streets and buildings. Manholes connect the sewer to the surface of the ground. Ready? Let's go—make sure you put the cover back on, or someone could fall in!

A SEWAGE WORKER ENTERS THROUGH THE MANHOLE.

IF SOMETHING GOES WRONG BELOW THE LIQUID SEWAGE LEVEL, A DIVER HAS TO GO DOWN AND FIX IT WEARING A LEAK-PROOF DIVING SUIT, HELMET, AND BREATHING GEAR.

A BRICK SEWER—BEAUTIFUL BUT STINKY!

SNIFF THAT SEWAGE

People who've been inside a working sewer say the smell is terrible, like a dirty toilet combined with dishwasher sludge, vomit, and eye-stinging noxious gases. A typical sewer contains a mixture of waste from showers, sinks, and toilets, along with rainwater, dirt, and litter from the streets. Everything that you pour down the drain or flush down the toilet ends up there. So a typical sewage soup includes unwanted drinks and food, poop, pee, toilet paper, vomit, head and body hair, snot, and lots of dirty water. Eau du Sewer, anyone?

HOME, SMELLY HOME

SEWERS AREN'T JUST FULL OF FILTH AND POOP— THEY'RE ALSO HOME TO SEVERAL KINDS OF ANIMALS.

* **RATS:** RATS ARE OMNIVORES WHO'LL EAT ALMOST ANYTHING, AND THEY LOVE WATER (RATS ARE GREAT SWIMMERS). SO SEWERS ALMOST ALWAYS HAVE A HEALTHY RAT POPULATION FEEDING ON THE LEFT-OVERS, FAT, AND POOP. DELIGHTFUL!

* **UNDERGROUND MOSQUITOES:** THERE REALLY IS A TYPE OF MOSQUITO CALLED THE UNDERGROUND MOSQUITO THAT LIVES IN SEWERS AND SUBWAY SYSTEMS AROUND THE WORLD. IN SEWERS, IT BITES AND FEEDS ON THE RATS, AND ANY HANDY HUMANS THAT HAPPEN TO PASS BY.

* **SPIDERS:** IN THE 1970S, TOKYO SEWAGE WORKERS SUPPOSEDLY FOUND A SPIDERWEB SO BIG AND STRONG THAT COCKROACHES AND EVEN RATS HAD BEEN CAUGHT IN IT! THEY NEVER SAW THE ACTUAL SPIDER ITSELF, THOUGH. LUCKY FOR THEM!

* **LOST IN THE SEWER:** MANY OTHER ANIMALS HAVE BEEN FOUND IN THE SEWERS AFTER GETTING LOST IN THERE. THEY'VE INCLUDED CATS, DOGS, SNAKES, GOLDFISH, FROGS, RACCOONS, FOXES, AND EVEN SHEEP. THEY'RE USUALLY VERY HAPPY TO BE RES-CUED BY SEWAGE WORKERS!

SEWER SURPRISE

A lot of the stuff in sewers is actually not supposed to be there at all, because it's not meant to be poured down the sink or flushed down the toilet. But people still do it, so sewers can also contain ...

* Used diapers
* Dental floss
* Cotton balls and pads
* Cat litter
* Used bandages
* Chewing gum
* Discarded medicine
* Cleaning wipes
* Paint
* Lumps of grease and hardened oil that have been used for cooking

These gross, often sticky discarded items can clump together and block underground sewage pipes. And trust us, you don't want that to happen— when blockages form, sewage can then "back up" and literally flow back up and out of the toilets and drains inside your home. Yuck!

A MONSTER FATBERG FOUND IN THE SEWERS OF LONDON, ENGLAND

FATBERG AHOY!

One of the worst problems in today's sewers is the dreaded "fatberg." Fatbergs are lumps of cooled, hardened cooking fat from homes and restau-rants, mixed with litter, food, and other unspeak-able sewage sludge. Some fatbergs are small, the size of a soccer ball or maybe a microwave. Others can get so huge they block whole sewer tunnels. Sewage workers have to go down and dig out the lumps of stinky, rotting grease bit by bit.

THE DISGUSTING TRUTH ABOUT DUST

YUCK-O-METER
EWW • GROSS • NASTY • DISGUSTING

LOOK UNDER YOUR BED, BEHIND THE TV, OR AROUND THE COUCH CUSHIONS, AND YOU'LL FIND THEM WAITING FOR YOU: BIG, GRAY, FLUFFY DUST BUNNIES. Yes, they sound cute, but a dust bunny might look more like a scary monster once you know what's inside it!

DUST CAN BE VISIBLE IN BEAMS OF LIGHT.

MAKING A MESS

You might think that when you breathe, you're breathing in pure, clear air. But air is not as clean as it looks. It's full of tons of tiny particles that are constantly breaking free from people, clothes, buildings, objects, and many other things. For a while, the particles float around in the air or are blown by the wind, but eventually they sink down, settle, and collect as dust. The dust gathers on the ground or on other flat surfaces, like shelves and the tops of doors. You can vacuum or wipe it away, but it still lurks in those hard-to-reach spots—and however much you clean it up, there's always more.

YOU CAN SEE HOW MUCH DUST IS FLOATING IN THE AIR BY LOOKING AT A FLASHLIGHT BEAM OR A SHAFT OF STRONG SUNLIGHT.

SOOT FROM FIRES

PIECES OF DEAD INSECTS

FOOD CRUMBS

FIBERS FROM MATERIALS

POLLEN

MUD AND SAND

MAKEUP

DEAD SKIN CELLS

DRIED-UP BOOGERS

DANDRUFF

SPECKS OF MOLD

OLD COBWEBS

SAWDUST

STRAY HAIRS

OLD EXOSKELETONS

DUST MITES ARE ARTHROPODS RELATED TO SPIDERS.

DIVE INTO DUST

What are all these bits? Well, it depends on where you are—indoors or outdoors, in a city or in the countryside—since dust is made of a mixture of all the materials and substances found in the surroundings. But a typical handful of dust, in a typical house, could contain ...

THE DUST IS ALIVE!

But it gets worse. Dust isn't made of just dead stuff; it also contains living things, like thousands of bacteria and other germs. Many fall off skin along with skin cells. And worse, some of the bacteria found in dust even come from poop! That's because tiny specks of poop escape when you flush the toilet, float around in the air, and eventually join the dust party.

Dust also contains huge numbers of creepy-crawlies. Want to see what they look like? Say hello to the dust mites that live in your dust bunnies, carpets, and mattresses ...

Dust mites feed mainly on dead skin, which is why they like hanging out in our furniture. But don't panic, you're not going to spot one—they're way too small for you to see! Dust mites don't bite, and most people aren't bothered by them. But if you'd like them to go away, it helps to leave your bed unmade. That lets fresh air inside, which dust mites don't like. (What a great excuse!)

ASH COATS EVERYTHING AFTER A VOLCANIC ERUPTION IN THE PHILIPPINES.

DEADLY DUST

DUST IS A PART OF LIFE, AND USUALLY NOT A BIG PROBLEM. BUT SOMETIMES IT CAN BE SERIOUSLY BAD NEWS AND EVEN CAUSE DISASTERS!

- MANY PEOPLE ARE ALLERGIC TO DUST MITE POOP OR TO PET HAIR AND DANDER. THEY NEED TO BUST DUST WITH POWERFUL VACUUMS AND USE SPECIAL SHEETS TO BLOCK DUST MITES.
- DUST CAN CONTAIN DANGEROUS ITEMS—SUCH AS CHEMICALS LIKE LEAD, PESTICIDES FROM FARMS, OR HARMFUL WASTE CHEMICALS FROM FACTORIES—THAT CAN MAKE PEOPLE SERIOUSLY SICK.
- AFTER A BIG VOLCANIC ERUPTION, VAST AMOUNTS OF VOLCANIC DUST MADE FROM PULVERIZED ROCK AND ASH CAN FILL THE SKY. AS IT SETTLES, IT COATS EVERYTHING IN A THICK DUSTY LAYER.

MAYBE FINDING A FEW DOMESTIC DUST BUNNIES ISN'T SO BAD AFTER ALL!

YOUR BUNNY'S DUST BUNNY

Do you have a pet, such as a dog, rabbit, or cat—or maybe all three? Uh-oh! Your dust is going to have even more grimy ingredients added to the mix: pet hairs, discarded whiskers and claws, muck from outdoors (or from litter trays), and dander, or animal skin flakes.

PUNGENT PEE

THE ROMANS USED PEE AS INVISIBLE INK. WHEN THE PAPER WAS HEATED UP, THE WIZ WRITING TURNED BROWN.

EWW • GROSS • NASTY • DISGUSTING

YUCK-O-METER

AS WE ALL KNOW, WHEN YOU HAVE TO GO, YOU HAVE TO GO! Twenty-four hours a day, the human body makes a steady drip, drip, drip of pee. Luckily, humans have a stretchy, baglike bladder used to store it until we can make it to a bathroom. But why? What is that yellow stuff made of, why does it smell ... and can people really drink it?

WHY WIZ?

READY TO BURST! YOU CAN SEE A BLADDER FULL OF PEE IN THIS X-RAY.

PEE, PEE-PEE, WIZ, OR URINE (TO USE A MORE SCIENTIFIC WORD) IS PART OF A CLEVER CLEANING SYSTEM THAT KEEPS YOUR BODY HEALTHY. As your cells work, they make waste chemicals, which pass into your blood. The blood then flows through your kidneys, two organs located in your lower back. They filter out the waste, along with some water, and the result is urine. If this didn't happen, your body would fill up with all the toxic waste chemicals—and gradually, they would start to make you sick.

Once your bladder is full, it sends signals to your brain to say, "Hey, time to head to the restroom!" Once you do, out whooshes a cup (240 mL) or more of pee. In a whole day, you'll produce about six cups (1.4 L) of urine. And in a whole lifetime, you could pee out 11,000 gallons (41,640 L)—enough to fill a small swimming pool (though you might not want to swim in it)!

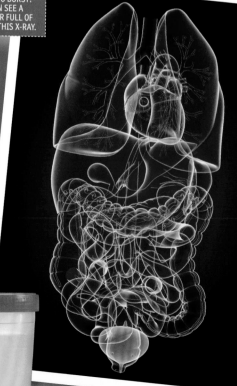

BE A WIZ **WHIZ**

DON'T TRY THIS AT HOME!

PEOPLE THROUGHOUT HISTORY HAVE HAD SOME STRANGE BELIEFS AND IDEAS ABOUT PEE—so let's get to the bottom of some of those urine-related myths. But don't try any of these at home!

CAN SOMEONE DRINK THEIR OWN PEE IF THEY'RE DYING OF THIRST IN THE DESERT? Well, yes, people can, and people have done it. Urine isn't usually poisonous, and drinking it can help people save water being lost by their body. In 1815, when Captain James Riley and his crew were shipwrecked and became lost in the Sahara, they ended up drinking not only their own pee but also camel pee!

However, the U.S. Army's survival guide says drinking urine is not a great idea, as it contains salty chemicals that can make humans more dehydrated. Instead, the official advice is to pee on a cloth and put it on your head to help you keep cool. Good thing no one's around!

IS URINE A HEALTH TONIC? Some people actually claim to drink a little of their own pee every day, because they think it has wonderful health benefits. But there's no evidence that this is true at all.

SHOULD YOU PEE ON A FRIEND'S JELLYFISH STING? No. There is an old rumor that urine somehow soothes jellyfish stings, but it's not true. For some types of jellyfish stings, vinegar helps. For others, hot water is better (as well as a trip to the hospital, as jellyfish stings can be serious). If someone is stung by a jellyfish, the best thing to do is consult a health professional.

IS URINE GOOD FOR SKIN? Well, sort of. One of the chemicals in pee is urea, which softens skin and helps to remove hard skin. Some baseball players claim to pee on their hands to prevent blisters and calluses. (But don't copy them ... you'll smell terrible!) You can also find urea in foot creams for smoothing rough skin.

PEE IS NOT THE SOLUTION TO A JELLYFISH STING.

WHAT'S THAT **SMELL?**

WHEN URINE IS FRESH, IT USUALLY DOESN'T SMELL VERY BAD. But if you've ever had to walk by a puddle of old pee you know that it smells gross. That's because the pee changes over time. Bacteria begin to break down the urea and turn it into much stronger, smellier ammonia.

However, after eating asparagus, some people's urine can come out smelling weird. This is because it includes chemicals that contain the stinky mineral sulfur, which add a strange whiff to their wiz.

CREEPY-CRAWLY CUISINE

HOW DO YOU FEEL ABOUT MUNCHING ON MOTHS? What about snacking on spiders? If you're gagging just imagining it, you're probably from a country or culture where slurping up insects is unusual and people find the very idea disgusting. However, in some parts of the world, bugs, grubs, and insects are seen as everyday eating, or even as delicious delicacies!

BUGGY BURGERS

Get ready, burger fans! If you ever visit the great lakes of eastern Africa, like Lake Victoria or Lake Malawi, you might see a very strange sight. Huge plumes of smoke seem to rise upward from the surface, coming straight out of the water. But this isn't smoke—it's millions and millions and millions of tiny flies. These insects, called midges, lay their eggs in the water and then emerge into the air when they become adults.

Around the shores of the lakes, the air soon fills with the tiny black flying pests. But instead of getting annoyed, the locals get ready for lunch! They take large pans, dampen them with water, then sweep them through the fly-filled air to gather up as many midges as they can. Then they roll handfuls of midges into juicy fly patties, grill or bake them, and serve them. Your order's up!

NOT A FIRE, JUST A FLY SWARM!

MIDGE BURGERS ARE **SUPER NUTRITIOUS** AND CONTAIN MORE THAN TWICE AS MUCH **PROTEIN** AS A HAMBURGER.

A DELICIOUS BOGONG MOTH

MOUTHWATERING MOTH

Hungry for more? Next on the menu is the plump, juicy bogong moth from Australia. Each year huge swarms of the moths migrate between the lowlands, where they feed, and the mountains, where they rest during the summer. In the past, different groups of Australia's Aboriginal peoples gathered during the migration to collect the moths, cook them on hot rocks, and enjoy enormous moth meals. The moths' bodies contain lots of fat to give them energy for their journey, so they're packed with calories—almost like nature's energy bars! This was very useful for people in the past, when there weren't always reliable sources of food.

On top of that, bogongs are well known for being irresistibly delicious. They are described as having a flavor between that of an almond and crispy pork cracklings. Though the traditional ceremonies no longer take place, the insects are so delicious that some chefs are creating new bogong recipes for their restaurants, such as moth frittatas or crispy fried moth. Who knows, maybe soon you'll be going bananas for bogongs!

IF YOU CAN'T BEAT 'EM, EAT 'EM!

EATING BUGS AND INSECTS IS A REALLY GOOD IDEA. THEY'RE NUTRITIOUS, EASY TO COOK, AND ARE OFTEN FOUND FLYING AROUND IN THE MILLIONS, FREE FOR THE TAKING! FOR EXAMPLE, SWARMS OF LOCUSTS OFTEN DESCEND ON FARMERS' CROPS AND STRIP THEM BARE. INSTEAD OF STARVING, IT MAKES SENSE TO JUST FRY UP THE LOCUSTS AND EAT THEM.

IN FACT, MANY EXPERTS THINK THAT, AS THE WORLD'S POPULATION INCREASES, CREEPY-CRAWLY CUISINE COULD BE THE ANSWER TO THE FOOD SHORTAGES OF THE FUTURE. SO IF YOU'RE STILL NOT SURE ABOUT FEASTING ON FLIES, MOTHS, OR GRASSHOPPERS, MAYBE IT'S TIME TO CHANGE YOUR MIND!

(HOWEVER, THAT DOESN'T MEAN YOU SHOULD GRAB THE FIRST BEETLE OR SPIDER YOU SEE AND GOBBLE IT—IT COULD BE CARRYING GERMS, OR HAVE A NASTY BITE. WAIT UNTIL SPECIALLY BRED AND COOKED VERSIONS ARE AVAILABLE IN THE GROCERY STORE!)

TASTY TARANTULAS

Is all this talk of eating midges and moths turning your stomach? Are you horrified and heaving at the thought of ingesting insects? Well, why not try a tarantula instead? They're very popular in Cambodia, where you'll often see street vendors carrying trays piled high with eight-legged snacks for sale.

Many Cambodians have a taste for creepy-crawlies; they also enjoy crickets and silkworms, a type of moth larva. The country's passion for crispy deep-fried spiders dates from times when food was scarce, and people turned to wild tarantulas to fill the gap. They have been a much loved delicacy ever since! They are cooked by sprinkling them with salt, sugar, or spices, and then frying them quickly in hot oil. The taste is said to be like a mixture of chicken and fish.

Go on … you know you want to!

SOME PEOPLE PREFER TO EAT ONLY THE TARANTULA'S CRUNCHY LEGS, WHICH TASTE A LOT LIKE CRAB, AND LEAVE THE ABDOMEN, AS IT CONTAINS THE SPIDER'S SLIMY INTERNAL ORGANS.

BARF-TASTIC BEAUTY TRENDS

HOW FAR WOULD YOU GO TO MAKE YOURSELF LOOK GOOD FOR A SELFIE? Would you paint yourself with deadly poison or beetle juice, or make a nice new pair of eyebrows from a dead mouse? How about smearing lard and flour all over your hair and not washing it for weeks? It sounds disgusting—and it is! But if you did all this a few hundred years ago, you'd be the belle of the ball.

YUCK-O-METER

EWW · GROSS · NASTY · DISGUSTING

WOMEN LIKE MARIE ANTOINETTE HAD TO USE SPECIAL TOOLS TO SCRATCH UNDER ALL THAT HAIR.

HORRID HAIRSTYLES

In Europe in the late 1700s, it became extremely fashionable for women to have huge hairstyles, reaching up to a foot (0.3 m) or even higher on top of their heads. They looked very impressive and were often decorated with ribbons, feathers, flowers, fruit, or even model birds.

But achieving this look wasn't easy. First, the hair had to be piled up on top of a wire frame, stuffed with pads of horsehair to make the 'do big enough. To hold it all in place, hairdressers covered the hair in lard (pig fat) to make it sticky. The fat-smeared hair mountain would then be dusted with powder, usually made from flour. As it took so much effort, a society lady would keep the same hairstyle for several weeks, even wearing it to bed!

Over that time, the grease and flour would start to rot, smelling terrible and attracting mice and insects. Fleas and lice would make their way inside the framework and nibble the lady's scalp, but she couldn't reach them. So people had special head-scratching sticks, which they could use to reach inside and give their itchy heads a rub. Anything for fashion!

U.S. PRESIDENT GEORGE WASHINGTON WORE THESE FALSE TEETH MADE FROM REAL HUMAN TEETH.

TERRIBLE TEETH

In the 1700s, people (at least, richer people) began to eat more sugary foods as they became more widely available. This damaged their teeth, which often became black and rotten. Once teeth were rotten, they had to be pulled out. In order to keep their grins fashionable, wealthy people had false teeth made of china or ivory (which came from elephants' tusks)—or even made of other people's teeth. In fact, one way for poor people to make some money was to sell their teeth to make false teeth for rich people. Even more unsettling, teeth were sometimes collected from dead bodies on battlefields to be used in sets of false teeth.

CREEPY COSMETICS TODAY

IF YOU THINK DISGUSTING BEAUTY TREATMENTS ARE ALL IN THE PAST, THINK AGAIN! THERE ARE ACTUALLY ALL KINDS OF GROSS AND GRUESOME INGREDIENTS IN MODERN MAKEUP AND COSMETICS TOO ...

- SPARKLY NAIL POLISH, EYE SHADOW, AND OTHER MAKEUP SOMETIMES CONTAIN GLITTER MADE FROM GROUND-UP FISH SCALES.

- SOME MOISTURIZERS ARE MADE USING SNAIL SLIME, AS IT HAS BEEN FOUND TO HELP MAKE SKIN SMOOTH AND SOFT. OR YOU CAN OPT FOR A SNAIL SLIME TREATMENT, WHERE LIVE SNAILS ARE ALLOWED TO CRAWL OVER YOUR SKIN.

- CRUSHED COCHINEAL BUGS ARE STILL USED TODAY IN SOME TYPES OF MAKEUP, AS WELL AS IN RED FOOD COLORING.

RED DYE WAS OFTEN MADE FROM COCHINEAL BUGS.

POISONOUS FACE PAINT

For the ancient Greeks, the ancient Romans, and people in Renaissance-era Europe, smooth and pale skin signaled high society and a life sheltered from working out in the sun. In order to achieve a superpale look, people smeared their faces with white makeup. Unfortunately, this makeup was often made from lead, a deadly poisonous metal. It scarred skin and even made people's hair fall out. People would then use even more lead makeup to cover up the damage—and too much of it could cause fatal lead poisoning.

To go with their white faces, people used the less deadly (but gorier) carmine—a red dye used to color lips and cheeks. And what was this beauty product made of? The crushed bodies of bright red cochineal bugs, a type of insect!

ATROCIOUS EYEBROWS

If you had no eyebrows left thanks to your lead makeup, you could wear mini eyebrow "wigs," cut from pieces of furry mouse skin and stuck onto your face with glue. By the end of a long evening of partying and dancing, ladies' mouse-skin eyebrows would sometimes fall off or slip downward—eek!

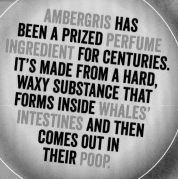

AMBERGRIS HAS BEEN A PRIZED PERFUME INGREDIENT FOR CENTURIES. IT'S MADE FROM A HARD, WAXY SUBSTANCE THAT FORMS INSIDE WHALES' INTESTINES AND THEN COMES OUT IN THEIR POOP.

ICKY, STICKY CHEWING GUM

GROSS NASTY DISGUSTING EWW
YUCK-O-METER

A LOT OF PEOPLE LOVE CHEWING GUM. If you do too, you might be wondering what it's doing in this book. It's just a tasty thing to put in your mouth, right?

But have you thought about what happens to your gum after you've chewed it and spit it out? If not, you'd better start now, because the world is facing a huge and gross chewed-up-gum problem. Thanks to gum's popularity, our poor planet is getting plastered in gazillions of globs of supersticky gunk, which then get stuck fast wherever they end up. That's not so sweet!

OOPS! I SWALLOWED IT!

YOU'VE PROBABLY HEARD THAT IF YOU SWALLOW CHEWING GUM, IT WILL STICK YOUR INSIDES TOGETHER, OR STAY INSIDE YOU FOR SEVEN YEARS. Luckily, that's false. It just comes out in your poop. However, people who swallow too much gum have been known to get a big sticky blockage in their guts, which has to be removed by surgery. You have been warned!

RUBBERY BUBBLES

THERE'S NOTHING NEW ABOUT WANTING TO CHEW— PEOPLE HAVE BEEN DOING IT FOR THOUSANDS OF YEARS. The ancient Greeks liked to chew a tree resin called mastic, while the Aztec and Maya chewed rubbery chicle tree gum.

In the 1860s, inventors added sugar and flavors to chicle, and modern chewing gum was born. In 1928, they created extra-stretchy gum, so that you could blow your spit-filled, mushed-up gum into a huge bubble that popped all over your face. Genius!

Gum is chewy and stretchy because of its "base"— the rubbery material it's made of. Today, gum-makers mostly use synthetic rubber instead of natural tree gum, so you're basically chewing a lump of soft, bendy, flavored plastic.

THIS ANCIENT WAD OF CHEWING GUM SHOWS JUST HOW LONG A PIECE OF GUM CAN STICK AROUND!

IN FINLAND, ARCHAEOLOGISTS HAVE FOUND 6,000-YEAR-OLD STONE AGE CHEWING GUM MADE FROM BIRCH TREE BARK.

A STICKY SITUATION

OF COURSE, EVERYONE READING THIS BOOK KNOWS YOU SHOULD WRAP USED CHEWING GUM UP AND PUT IT IN THE TRASH. But some people don't do that! They spit their germy, gunky gum out onto roads, sidewalks, and floors—or sneakily stick it somewhere, like under a desk, café table, or bus or subway seat. And all this causes a lot of gross, gummy problems.

- Gum is super sticky—it has to be, so that it won't fall apart when you chew it. After it's spat out, it gets hard, and sticks like glue.

- The cities of the world have countless globs of gum splatted all over the ground. It soon gets dirty, so it forms black spots. They're incredibly difficult and expensive to clean off.

- Freshly chewed gum can gross out anyone who steps in it, or finds it stuck to their seat or table. Once gum is in your clothes or hair, it can be impossible to get out.

EACH GUM SPLAT HAS TO BE INDIVIDUALLY BLASTED OFF WITH A HIGH-POWERED STEAM JET.

GETTING RID OF GROSS GUM

WHAT CAN BE DONE ABOUT THE GUM THREATENING TO ENGULF OUR STREETS? LOTS OF THINGS!

GUM CRIME
IN SINGAPORE, IT'S SIMPLE: JUST MAKE CHEWING GUM ILLEGAL! YOU'RE ALLOWED TO BUY IT ONLY IF IT'S BEEN PRESCRIBED BY A PHARMACIST. MEANWHILE, OTHER CITIES ARE BRINGING IN BIG FINES FOR ANYONE CAUGHT GUM-LITTERING.

GULP THAT GUM!
MEXICO'S GOVERNMENT GOT SO FED UP WITH CLEANING UP GUM, IT TOLD THE COUNTRY'S CITIZENS TO SIMPLY SWALLOW IT INSTEAD. WHAT COULD POSSIBLY GO WRONG? (SEE TO THE LEFT.)

GUM ART?
IF YOU CAN'T BEAT IT, MAKE IT BEAUTIFUL! GUM ARTISTS HAVE BEGUN TURNING EACH SPLAT OF GUM INTO A MINI-ARTWORK, PAINTED IN BRIGHT COLORS.

GUM ALLEYS
IN SOME CITIES, PEOPLE HAVE BEGUN STICKING GUM ALL OVER PARTICULAR STREETS OR WALLS, WHICH BECOME COLORFUL TOURIST ATTRACTIONS. SEATTLE, WASHINGTON, U.S.A., HAS A GUM WALL, WHILE SAN LUIS OBISPO IN CALIFORNIA, U.S.A., HAS A BUBBLEGUM ALLEY.

THE GROSSEST GUM HABITS

IF YOU'RE GOING TO CHEW GUM, AT LEAST REMEMBER YOUR MANNERS! When interviewed, gum chewers have admitted to some truly revolting behavior, such as …

- Spitting gum out to eat, then putting the cold, chewed lump back in their mouth later.

- Keeping a lump of gum BEHIND THEIR EAR until they want to chew it again!

- SHARING chewed gum with other people! Ewwwwwww!

- Making gross snapping and squelching noises that drive other people mad.

GUM ART IN LONDON, ENGLAND

This Is Your
Happy Place

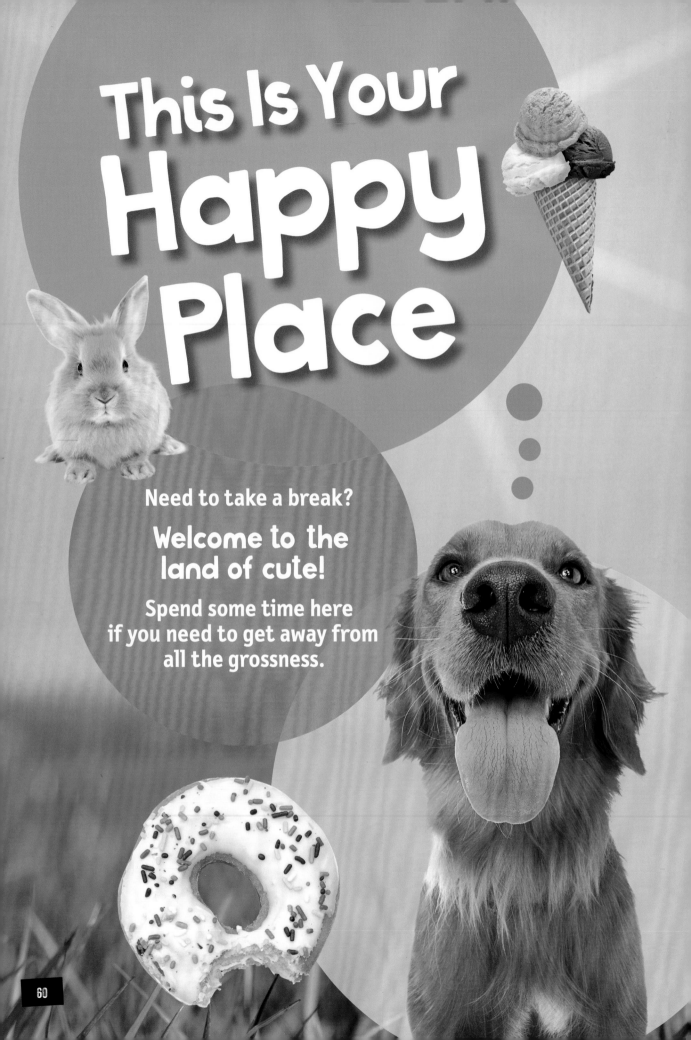

Need to take a break?

Welcome to the land of cute!

Spend some time here if you need to get away from all the grossness.

MONSTROUS MOLD!

YUCK-O-METER

EWW • GROSS • NASTY • DISGUSTING

WANT SOME JELLY ON YOUR TOAST? Suddenly not feel-ing hungry? But why? Could it be that gross black-ish, greenish, furry growth all over it? This yucky, fluffy coating is a sure sign that your jelly has seen better days and has now succumbed to an attack of MOLD ... which means it would definitely be a terrible idea to eat it!

HUNGRY FUNGI

Foods like sandwiches, pastries, and fruit will grow mold if they're left lying around for long enough. But what is that freaky fuzz? Just like us humans, molds are living things. They are a type of fungi, related to mushrooms and yeast. And like all living things, they need food. When you find a jar of jam covered in mold, that's because the mold is eating the jam (hey, finders keepers!).

The scary truth is that mold is EVERYWHERE—just roaming around in the air, waiting for something to land on. Because one sandwich is not enough for those molds—they want to spread out as far as they can and feed on whatever they can find. As molds grow, they release tiny seedlike spores into the surroundings. In fact, the air in an aver-age kitchen contains thousands of miniature mold spore invaders, from dozens of different mold species.

When a mold spore settles on food, such as a slice of bread, it grabs its chance to put down roots, grow, and take over your lunch! It sprouts tiny roots, called rhizoids, that reach down into the bread to feed. Then it grows sticking-up hairlike parts called fruiting bodies that create that revolting furry, fluffy, or powdery look. And their job is? ... to release even more spores!

MOLD

SPORES BEING RELEASED

FRUITING BODIES

RHIZOIDS, OR ROOTS

THIS IS WHY KEEPING FOOD WELL WRAPPED IS A GOOD IDEA. EVEN IF IT'S IN THE REFRIGERATOR, MOLD SPORES CAN GET THROUGH THE DOORS!

SOME MOLD CAN BE HARMFUL.

FUZZY PHOBIA

Some people aren't scared even a bit by mold growing on their cheese or jam. They just scrape it off and eat the rest! "Don't be such a wuss!" they cry as they chow down. Is that really OK? Well, it depends on the mold species. Some are harmless. But it's a good idea to avoid mold if you can, as a few species can be dangerous—even deadly. A type of mold that grows on grains and nuts can make you super sick. Breathing in mold spores is dangerous too, as they can damage the insides of your lungs. If you find clouds of mold spores in a trash can or garden shed, for example—hold your breath and back away!

MOLD ON THE MENU

As with so many of the "disgusting" things in this book, some people consider mold a delicious delicacy. In fact, eating mold is pretty normal for most of us. Ever tried blue cheese, or white-rind cheeses like brie and Camembert? Then you're a mold muncher! Fortunately, these types of mold are pretty safe.

THE BLUE STREAKS IN BLUE CHEESE ARE MOLD THAT'S DELIBERATELY ADDED TO THE CHEESE AS IT'S MADE TO GIVE IT A SHARP, TANGY TASTE.

THE WHITE RIND ON SOFT CHEESES LIKE BRIE IS A TYPE OF EDIBLE MOLD.

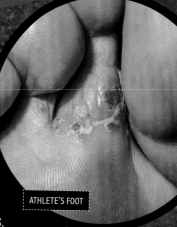

ATHLETE'S FOOT

MORE MOLD

BESIDES GROWING ON OUR FOOD, MOLD CAN BE FOUND IN PLENTY OF OTHER PLACES TOO …

○ MOLDS LOVE MOISTURE. (THAT'S WHY THEY GROW ON FRUIT AND BREADS, AND NOT SO MUCH ON DRY PASTA OR FLOUR.) STEAMY BATHROOMS ARE THE PERFECT HOME FOR MOLDS THAT GROW ON SHOWER CURTAINS, SOGGY BATH MATS, AND TILE GROUT. BLACK BATHROOM MOLD IS BAD NEWS, AS IT CAN TRIGGER ASTHMA.

○ SOME MOLDS LIKE TO FEED ON OTHER LIVING THINGS—INCLUDING YOUR FEET! ATHLETE'S FOOT IS A TYPE OF CRUSTY, FLAKY, SCALY MOLD THAT GROWS BETWEEN PEOPLE'S TOES, DEVOURING DAMP SKIN.

○ THERE ARE EVEN MOLDS THAT MUNCH WOOD, PLASTIC, ROCK, AND METAL!

QUIZ

GROSSBUSTERS!

ARE YOU ARMED WITH THE KNOWLEDGE, COURAGE, AND SHEER GUTS to deal with the most sickening scenarios that life can throw at you? Do you know what to do when faced with a disgusting toilet blockage, a creepy cockroach, or even worse, a moldy cupcake?

Well, we're not going to take your word for it. Instead, take this test to reveal the truth! You might find some of the answers you need in the pages of this book. For others, you'll have to rely on your own wits, common sense, and gross-busting instincts. Ready to face the most revolting quiz questions of all time?

3 YOU'RE ABOUT TO EAT A DELICIOUS-LOOKING SANDWICH IN A CAFÉ, WHEN A COCKROACH RUNS ACROSS YOUR FOOT! YOU ...

A. Catch that roach and pop it in your sandwich—it's protein after all!

B. Ignore it. Who cares, it's just a cockroach!

C. Return the sandwich—this café isn't very clean!

D. Scream, overturn the table, and run for your life.

1 YOU'RE CRAVING A CUPCAKE, BUT THERE'S ONLY ONE LEFT, AND ... OH, NO ... IT'S COVERED IN FUZZY GREEN MOLD! WHAT DO YOU DO?

A. Scrape the mold off and stir it into some soft cheese. It might taste great!

B. Take a good sniff to check if it really is mold, or just strange-colored frosting.

C. Hold your breath, wrap up the cake, throw it in the trash, and wash your hands.

D. Evacuate the house and call the fire department immediately.

4 YOU'VE JUST GOTTEN A SMALL CUT ON YOUR FINGERTIP AND IT'S STARTED TO BLEED. SHOULD YOU ...

A. Collect the blood to look at under a microscope?

B. Wash and dry the cut, then put on a bandage?

C. Bandage it as tightly as possible?

D. Suck your finger to get the blood out?

2 YOU'RE AT SCHOOL, AND YOU SUDDENLY FEEL LIKE YOU'RE ABOUT TO BARF. YOUR NEXT STEP?

A. Tell an adult and ask to go home as soon as possible.

B. Grab your friend and ask them to have a look down your throat.

C. Try to hold it down and hope for the best.

D. Hurl quietly into a potted plant. Tell no one.

5 OH NO! THE TOILET IS BLOCKED WITH A POOP OF GINORMOUS PROPORTIONS. HOW DO YOU FIX IT?

A. Put your hand down the toilet to push that poop on its way.

B. Use a coat hanger to mash and break the poop up, so it will flush more easily.

C. Pour some liquid soap into the toilet, followed by a pail or large jug of warm water.

D. Kick the toilet a few times—that should dislodge it!

6 A HUGE RED ZIT HAS APPEARED ON YOUR CHIN OVERNIGHT. WHAT'S THE BEST PLAN OF ACTION?

A. Squeeze it as hard as you can until it pops.

B. Press it gently with a hot, damp facecloth.

C. Cover it with toothpaste.

D. Slather it with makeup.

7 THERE'S A GRUMPY-LOOKING SKUNK IN YOUR GARDEN, AND IT MIGHT BE ABOUT TO SPRAY. YOU …

A. Scare it away by playing the loudest musical instrument you have.

B. Throw leaves at it. It will think it's in the forest and calm down.

C. Sprinkle some lemon peel around the garden. Skunks hate the smell and will run away.

D. Switch on a bright light, and the skunk will probably leave.

8 YOUR FRIEND PICKED A MUSHROOM IN THE WOODS, AND SHE WANTS TO TAKE IT HOME TO COOK. WHAT DO YOU SAY?

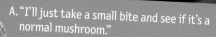

A. "I'll just take a small bite and see if it's a normal mushroom."

B. "Wait, let me check in this woodland spotter's guide to see what it is."

C. "No way—it might be deadly!"

D. "Don't eat it—let's take it to school for the nature collection instead."

9 YOU FIND STRANGE LITTLE CYLINDER-SHAPED BLACK THINGS IN THE COOKIE JAR. YOU …

A. Eat them … they're probably just chocolate chips, right?

B. Throw them out.

C. Throw them out, along with the cookies.

D. Throw them out, along with the cookies and the cookie jar.

10 A GIANT SPIDER JUMPS OUT OF A BUNCH OF BANANAS IN YOUR FRUIT BOWL. YOUR REACTION?

A. Run out of the room and call for help.

B. Leave it alone so it can kill flies and bugs around the house.

C. Try to catch it in a jar.

D. Pick it up.

ANSWERS:

1. C)
Hold your breath, wrap up the cake, throw it in the trash, and wash your hands. It's probably fine, but avoid breathing in mold, just in case it's harmful. It's true some molds can be eaten, but you don't know if this is one of them!

2. A)
Tell an adult and ask to go home as soon as possible. You may have germs that could spread the sickness around the school. It's best to stay at home for at least two days.

3. C)
Return the sandwich—this café isn't very clean! Seeing one cockroach means there are probably more nearby—possibly in the kitchen. Insects are a high-protein food, but eating a dirty, wild cockroach really isn't a good idea.

4. B)
Wash and dry the cut, then put on a bandage. Bandaging too tightly could cut off the blood to your fingertip, but a cut does need to be kept clean and covered. Sucking it could put germs from your mouth in the cut.

5. C)
Pour some liquid soap into the toilet, followed by a pail or large jug of warm water. This should help to push the problem poop along without you having to go near it! (As long as the toilet isn't overflowing, of course.)

6. B)
Press it gently with a hot, damp facecloth. Using a hot cloth is the quickest way to help drain that zit.

7. D)
Switch on a bright light, and the skunk will probably leave. Skunks hate bright lights. Citrus peel can help keep them away too, but if a skunk is already there, try to stay out of its way.

8. C)
"No way—it might be deadly!" Even people who thought they knew what they were doing have been harmed by dangerous fungi that look normal. Don't risk it!

9. C)
Throw them out, along with the cookies. If you find something like this, it's probably mouse poop. The cookies have to go, but the cookie jar will be OK with a good washing.

10. A)
Run out of the room and call for help. Most everyday house spiders are harmless and do catch flies. But a big spider in your bananas could be a deadly Brazilian wandering spider that's accidentally been shipped along with the fruit. (Unlikely, but possible.) Run away!

HOW DID YOU DO?

1–3 CORRECT ANSWERS
Who you gonna call? Well, sadly, not you … yet! Keep reading, and you'll be an expert in no time.

4–7 CORRECT ANSWERS
Not too shabby! You can handle a selection of gross scenarios with aplomb, but there's always room for improvement.

8–10 CORRECT ANSWERS
Who you gonna call? You, of course—because you're the Grossbuster General!

BLOOD-CURDLING!

YUCK-O-METER

EWW · GROSS · NASTY · DISGUSTING

BLOOD IS ESSENTIAL FOR LIFE, AND ALL OF US HAVE IT FLOWING AROUND INSIDE OUR BODIES. So why do some people throw up or faint when they see a tiny drop?

BLECH—BLOOD!

Actually, it's natural to get slightly woozy at the sight of blood. If you see someone's blood, that probably means they've been injured, and there might be some kind of violence or danger nearby. In prehistoric times, for example, it could warn you that there was a dangerous animal around, like a saber-toothed tiger. So it makes sense that we instinctively feel a little panicked when we see bleeding and injuries. In some folks, that reaction is extra strong, and they just can't look at blood at all!

IF THIS IS YOU, MAKE SURE YOU'RE SITTING DOWN TO READ THIS SECTION. IT COULD MAKE YOUR BLOOD RUN COLD!

BOUNTIFUL BLOOD

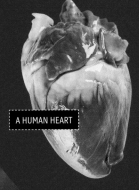

A HUMAN HEART

To do its job of delivering oxygen, food, and chemicals all over your body, blood has to circulate, or flow around and around. To make this happen, the heart squeezes, pumping the blood through the blood vessels, or tubes. This means the blood is under pressure. If you get a cut or wound, the pressure makes the blood flow—or even squirt—out.

In fact, the heart pumps SO hard that if it weren't inside the body, it could squirt blood a distance of 30 feet (10 m)!

A SCAB GETS DRIER AND DARKER AND THEN FINALLY FALLS OFF ONCE THE SKIN HAS HEALED—AS LONG AS YOU DON'T PICK IT, THAT IS!

WHEN BLOOD TRANSFUSIONS WERE FIRST INVENTED IN THE 1600S, DOCTORS GAVE BLOOD FROM ANIMALS INSTEAD OF HUMANS.

SCAB SAVIORS

Bleeding a little can be helpful, as it washes germs out of cuts. But you don't want to bleed a lot, as you could lose too much of the blood you need to stay alive. Luckily, healthy blood soon starts to clot—that is, clump and stick together to form a plug and stop any more blood from escaping. As the clot dries, it hardens into a crispy, crusty scab. Now, scabs are a great thing. They stop you from bleeding and they keep your cut safely covered while the skin underneath heals over. Yet many people find scabs unbearably revolting! This could be because diseases such as chickenpox and smallpox involve being covered in scabs, so they could be seen as a sign of disease and germs.

WHEN MONKEYS GROOM EACH OTHER, THEY PICK AND EAT EACH OTHER'S SCABS (ALONG WITH LICE AND SKIN FLAKES). IT'S PERFECTLY NATURAL— BUT DON'T TRY THIS AT HOME!

SCABBY SNACKS

Scabs can be horribly itchy, and some people just can't resist picking at them. Of course, that's a bad idea, as it delays the healing process. Just be patient, and wait until your scabs fall off.

And you certainly wouldn't eat a scab. Would you? Well, it's not unheard of. In fact, it's saintly! Saint Angela of Foligno, who lived in 13th-century Italy, often looked after people suffering from leprosy, which causes sores and scabs. Angela described how she washed a victim's feet and then drank the washing water, swallowing a scab. Doing this was considered especially holy and devoted!

Eating scabs could even save your life. In 2003, a British man was kidnapped in Colombia, but he escaped and wandered in the jungle for days with nothing to eat. He had several wounds from his ordeal, so he picked the scabs off and ate them as snacks!

BEAUTIFUL RED BLOOD

THIS PHOTO SHOWS THE BLUE BLOOD OF HORSE-SHOE CRABS BEING COLLECTED. IT'S USED TO MAKE A TEST TO DETECT GERMS ON MEDICAL EQUIPMENT.

ONE THING ANYONE CAN TELL YOU ABOUT BLOOD IS THAT IT'S RED. OR IS IT? WELL, IT IS IF YOU'RE A HUMAN, OR A VERTEBRATE ANIMAL, LIKE A DOG, A LIZARD, OR A WHALE. RED BLOOD CONTAINS IRON, WHICH HELPS IT TO WORK, AND IRON-BASED CHEMICALS ARE USUALLY RED. HOWEVER, SOME ANIMALS HAVE BLOOD OF A DIFFERENT COLOR INSTEAD.

- OCTOPUSES, SPIDERS, AND CRABS HAVE BLUE BLOOD, WHICH CONTAINS COPPER INSTEAD OF IRON.
- SOME LEECHES AND WORMS HAVE GREEN BLOOD.
- BUTTERFLIES AND OTHER INSECTS HAVE PALE WHITE OR YELLOWISH BLOOD.
- SOME SEA WORMS HAVE PURPLE BLOOD.
- MOST FISH HAVE RED BLOOD, BUT THE AMAZING ANTARCTIC ICEFISH HAS LOST ITS RED BLOOD CELLS. ITS BLOOD IS CLEAR AND COLORLESS, LIKE THE FISH ITSELF!

SOME ICEFISH ALSO HAVE TRANSPARENT BODIES.

WADS OF WORMS

GROSS NASTY DISGUSTING EWW

YUCK-O-METER

THERE ARE THOUSANDS OF DIFFERENT SPECIES OF WORMS, AND THEY'RE NOT ALL PEACEFUL SOIL-MUNCHERS THAT ARE HELP-FUL TO GARDENERS. The gross and gruesome worms on this page are parasites, which can sometimes invade peo-ple's bodies and live inside them. They have clever and cunning adaptations, and some of them look like monsters from outer space! These sneaky slitherers are just a few of the body-invading worms to watch out for ...

ITCHY Invasion

These threadworms might not look too scary—they're just like tiny threads, right? But get ready to gag—their life cycle is *gross*. Thread-worms invade when a person accidentally gets worm eggs in their mouth. The eggs hatch and the worms live in the person's intestines. Finally, they exit through the victim's rear, where the female worms lay thousands *more* tiny eggs that make people awfully itchy.

When a person's rear gets so itchy, some people can't help but scratch—especially young children. As they scratch, tiny worm eggs get stuck under their fingernails. The eggs then end up on food or other things that the person touches, where they can spread to other kids' hands and mouths—and the cycle starts again.

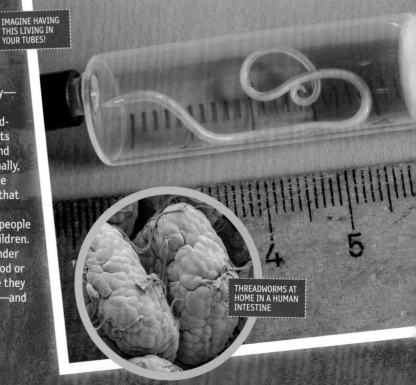

IMAGINE HAVING THIS LIVING IN YOUR TUBES!

THREADWORMS AT HOME IN A HUMAN INTESTINE

HORRIBLE Hookworms

Feel like taking a stroll? Hookworms usually enter the human body through bare feet. The baby hookworms, called larvae, hang out in the soil in warm, damp areas. When a bare foot passes by, they hang on and then burrow into the skin. Once inside, a baby hookworm moves into the blood vessels, travels to the lungs, and worms its way up into the victim's throat, where the victim—get ready for this—swallows it. It passes through the stomach and finally arrives at its destination, the intestines.

Here's where the "hook" part comes in. The larva grows into an adult that hooks itself on to the inside of the victim's intestines, using its terrible toothy face. It feeds on blood, and it lays eggs that come out in the person's poop. If there isn't a modern sewage system, the eggs and larvae end up back in the ground, ready for the next bare foot!

But don't panic too much. You're unlikely to catch a hookworm, and even if you did, hospitals have medicines to get rid of it. Phew!

THE HOOKWORM USES ITS HOOKLIKE TEETH TO HANG ON TO THE INTESTINE WALL.

Tapeworm TERROR

Humans can catch tapeworm eggs by eating undercooked meat, such as pork, beef, or fish, or by drinking dirty water. Like a hookworm, the adult tapeworm attaches to the intestines. As a person's chewed-up dinner flows past, the tapeworm soaks up food through its skin. It keeps forming new, flat body sections, making it look like a long ribbon, or tape. At the bottom end, sections filled with eggs break off and come out in the infected person's waste, spreading the eggs into the soil or water supply, to be swallowed by animals or humans.

A beef tapeworm, which can be caught by eating undercooked beef, can grow to more than 50 feet (15 m) long—yes, that's while living inside someone. And it can stay there, holding on tight and dropping its egg-filled packages, for 25 years. When a worm finally dies, the whole thing comes out in the person's poop. *Ewww!*

TAPEWORMS HAVE A RING OF HOOKS ON THEIR HEADS FOR GRIPPING YOUR GUTS.

GOOD NEWS, BAD NEWS

GOOD NEWS
YOU'LL BE HAPPY TO HEAR THAT THERE ARE MEDICINES THAT CAN ZAP MOST OF THESE SQUIRMY INVADERS DEAD, SIMPLY AND EASILY. THANK GOODNESS! AND WE MAY SOON BE ABLE TO SAY GOODBYE TO THE GUINEA WORM, THANKS TO A HUGE HEALTH CAMPAIGN THAT'S GRADUALLY GETTING RID OF IT.
BAD NEWS
UNFORTUNATELY, IN SOME COUNTRIES THERE AREN'T ENOUGH ANTI-WORM MEDICINES. THIS MEANS WORM ATTACKS OFTEN AREN'T TREATED, AND MILLIONS OF PEOPLE HAVE TO LIVE WITH WORMS IN THEIR BODIES. THEY CAN CAUSE STOMACHACHES, HEADACHES, TIREDNESS, AND OTHER PROBLEMS.

THE Gruesome Guinea Worm

This scary worm, found in parts of Africa, is luckily pretty rare. Its larvae live in water, and if they are accidentally swallowed, they end up in people's intestines. But the adult worms don't stay there—instead, they break out through the intestine walls. The female worm, which can grow to over four feet (1.2 m) long, heads toward the skin of the leg or foot. A burning, stinging blister appears, which usually causes the infected person to stick their leg in cold water. The female then emerges to lay thousands of eggs in the water.

THE ONLY WAY TO GET A GUINEA WORM OUT IS TO WRAP ONE END OF IT AROUND A TWIG OR MATCHSTICK, AND GENTLY PULL IT OUT, LITTLE BY LITTLE.

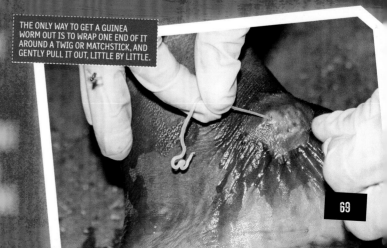

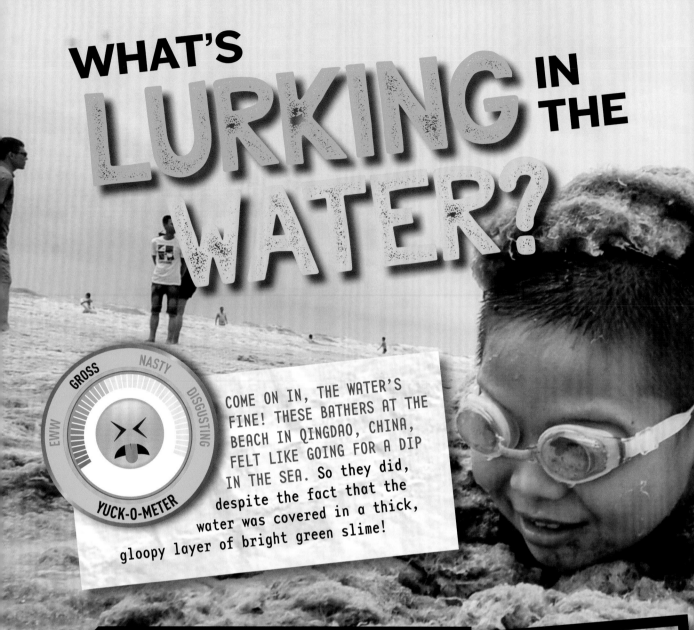

WHAT'S LURKING IN THE WATER?

YUCK-O-METER

EWW · GROSS · NASTY · DISGUSTING

COME ON IN, THE WATER'S FINE! THESE BATHERS AT THE BEACH IN QINGDAO, CHINA, FELT LIKE GOING FOR A DIP IN THE SEA. So they did, despite the fact that the water was covered in a thick, gloopy layer of bright green slime!

SICKENING SLIME

It may look like something out of a sci-fi movie, but this shocking sea slime is actually a common living thing that you've seen many times before: algae. Algae are plantlike organisms that come in a range of sizes, from leafy sea-weeds to single-celled creatures that form mats or clumps of slime. Algae is the green stuff that grows in a dirty fish tank and fills garden ponds with slimy, stringy pondweed.

In Qingdao, the green slime invasion happens every summer, thanks to a combination of seaweed farming, water pollution, warm temperatures, and sunlight on the sea surface. The algae quickly grow and spread over the sea, and then are blown toward the shore and pile up. Algae are harmless to humans, so instead of running away screaming, people have now started to enjoy the annual slime-fest. Locals and tourists gather to swim in it and cover their bodies with it for photos.

GREEN ALGAE POND SLIME GIVES THIS FROG GREAT CAMOUFLAGE!

TOXIC TERROR

The bad news is that algal blooms—large populations of algae—aren't always harmless fun. Some species of algae release toxic chemicals into the water that can kill animals, such as dolphins. Some just block out the sun, making it hard for sea creatures below the surface to survive. Algal blooms can also poison shellfish, which in turn poison anyone who eats them. And when a huge mass of algae dies and starts to rot, it can release nasty gases that smell terrible and even make it hard to breathe.

ALGAE AREN'T THE ONLY CREATURES THAT CAN BLOOM. A "JELLYFISH BLOOM" IS A JELLYFISH POPULATION EXPLOSION, WHEN VAST NUMBERS OF FLOATING JELLIES COLLECT IN ONE PLACE.

NOT IN THE SEA, PLEASE!

Perhaps the grossest thing in the sea is what doesn't belong there—pollution. Chemicals used on land, especially farm fertilizers, end up being washed into rivers by the rain, and then flowing out to sea. The point of them is to make plants grow better, which is great news for farmers. But in the oceans, they make seaweeds and algae go crazy! Their explosive growth can create a clogged, gloomy underwater scene. The oxygen in the water gets used up, and it's hard for other creatures to survive.

And if you go swimming or surfing in the sea, you might be in for a shock when you come face to face with human poop! Many coastal cities and villages dump waste into the sea, especially if they don't have modern sewage plants. In the water, the poop breaks up or gets snacked on by sea creatures. But it also washes ashore, where it can make beaches super smelly.

GROSS WATERY GRAVEYARDS

WHEN SEA CREATURES DIE, THEY SINK DOWN TO THE BOTTOM OF THE OCEAN TO BECOME A ROTTING FEAST FOR HAGFISH (SEE PAGES 42–43) AND OTHER SEABED SCAVENGERS. BUT BEFORE THAT, A DEAD WHALE, SQUID, OR OTHER ANIMAL CAN SOMETIMES FILL WITH GASES AS ITS BODY ROTS. THE GASES MAKE IT FLOAT FOR A WHILE. DURING THAT TIME, THE BODIES SOMETIMES FLOAT ASHORE. THAT'S WHAT HAPPENED WHEN THIS HUGE OBJECT WAS SPOTTED FLOATING AROUND IN THE SEA NEAR AUSTRALIA. IT TURNED OUT TO BE A DEAD HUMPBACK WHALE WITH ITS HUGE, STRETCHY THROAT BLOWN UP LIKE A BALLOON BY GASES INSIDE ITS BODY.

A BLOATED HUMPBACK WHALE WASHED ASHORE.

VILE VOMIT

NASTY

GROSS

EWW

DISGUSTING

YUCK-O-METER

BLEEEUUURRRGGHH! Puking your guts up when you're sick has to be one of the grossest experiences there is. It tastes and smells terrible, it sounds even worse, and when it gets stuck in your teeth, your nose, or even your hair—ewww! So why do our bodies put us through something so revolting when we're already feeling unwell? Like so many gross body behaviors, there's a practical reason for puking!

REJECTED!!!

Your body is like a finely tuned machine—certain things help it function, and others gum up the works. Too much sugary food or fizzy soda? No good. Food that contains mold, dangerous bacteria, or something you're allergic to? Even worse. That gross, queasy feeling you get when you just know you're going to throw up actually means your body is taking steps to protect you from something bad. Hurling it all up may be horrible and stinky, but it could save you from a serious illness.

When you have a stomach bug, it means some germs, such as salmonella bacteria, have managed to get in and stay in. But it's not the germs that cause you to spew chunks—it's actually your body's very own defense mechanism! You keep on barfing over and over, because your body is trying to get rid of the foreign invaders. The same thing happens at the other end too—your body tries to poop out those bugs by giving you diarrhea!

MANY PEOPLE GET **MOTION SICKNESS** WHEN THEY FLY, AND IN SPACE. HURLING IN SPACE COULD GET MESSY, SO ASTRONAUTS ON THE INTERNATIONAL SPACE STATION HAVE SPECIAL BARF BAGS TO USE.

BARFING: THE BASICS

So how does puking actually happen? Like sneezing, once it's under way, your body takes over, and it's very hard to control it. And apart from being disgusting, it's actually amazingly clever. As you sprint to the bathroom, your body goes through a brilliantly timed sequence of steps to prepare to puke:

1. DROOLING
You make extra saliva to protect your teeth from the stomach acid and to help expel the barf.

2. GOING GREEN
You look pale or greenish as the blood drains from your face. That's because it's all headed to the stomach muscles, to help them do their job.

3. GASPING
You gasp to take in extra oxygen to help power the puke, and also to make sure you can't breathe in while puking (as that could make you choke).

4. SQUEE-EEE-EEZING
You retch and double over as your stomach muscles cramp and squeeze as hard as they can, forcing the contents of your stomach up into your throat.

5. RELEASING THE BARF!
Finally, the top of your throat opens, so that everything can come shooting out at high speed.

THIS FOSSILIZED BARF IS FULL OF SEASHELLS. IT IS THOUGHT TO HAVE BEEN PUKED UP BY A SEA REPTILE CALLED AN ICHTHYOSAUR.

WHEW, THAT'S BETTER!

Right after upchucking, you usually feel a lot better. This is because the process releases brain chemicals called endorphins that make you relieved and happy. Your muscles relax and the nausea goes away (until next time, that is).

On the downside, the sight of you puking could set someone else off. When people see, hear, or smell someone else throwing up, they sometimes end up doing it themselves as well. This is called "sympathy vomiting," and there could be a good reason for it. In prehistoric times, when most humans lived in small groups and collected their food from the wild, everyone in the village would share the same dinner. If one person threw it up, it made sense for others to vomit as soon as possible, in case they had all eaten the same poison.

BRAIN BARF

SOME PEOPLE HAVE STRONGER STOMACHS THAN OTHERS. DO YOU RALPH ON ROLLER COASTERS?

BUT HANG ON ONE SECOND. WHAT ABOUT ALL THOSE OTHER TIMES YOU THROW UP, OR FEEL LIKE YOU'RE ABOUT TO? WHAT ABOUT WHEN YOU'VE JUST CLIMBED OFF A HIGH-SPEED AMUSEMENT PARK RIDE, OR FEEL SICK WITH NERVES WHEN YOU'RE ABOUT TO GO ON STAGE? OR WHEN YOU FEEL ILL EVEN JUST RIDING IN A CAR? CLEARLY, IN THOSE CASES, NOTHING HAS ACTUALLY POISONED YOU.

SCIENTISTS THINK THIS TYPE OF VOMITING COULD BE A CASE OF A MIX-UP IN YOUR BRAIN. WHEN YOU GET DIZZY, OR SEE THE WORLD WHIZZING BY AT HIGH SPEED, YOUR BRAIN MISINTERPRETS THIS, AND IT DECIDES YOU MUST BE SUFFERING FROM THE EFFECTS OF POISONING. WHEN YOU GET A SUDDEN SHOCK, OR FEEL REALLY SCARED, IT CAN CHANGE YOUR BLOOD PRESSURE AND THE BALANCE OF CHEMICALS IN YOUR BODY—ANOTHER THING THAT CAN HAPPEN WHEN YOU ARE POISONED. SO, JUST TO BE ON THE SAFE SIDE, THE BRAIN TRIGGERS THE BARFING PROCESS.

FREAKY FLAVORS TO SAVOR

GROSS NASTY DISGUSTING EWW

YUCK-O-METER

WHAT'S THE LEAST APPETIZING POTATO CHIP FLAVOR YOU CAN IMAGINE? What about things that should never be made into ice cream? Whatever you're thinking of, you might find it actually exists! Here you'll discover some of the oddest, grossest, and most disgusting snack flavors ever created. And hey, maybe you should try some—a lot of them are really popular!

WALKERS™

Cajun Squirrel
flavour potato crisps

Do you have a flavour
PICK US
WINNER!

VOTE FOR ME!

This picture represents Martin from his inspiration for his Cajun Squirrel Flavour

70g pack contains:
Sugar 1.6g 2% | Fat 15.0g 21% | Saturates 1.2g 6% | Salt 0.58g 10%

WACKY CHIPS AROUND THE WORLD

As we've learned, different countries around the world have their own local delicacies, and some folks enjoy flavors that others find disgustingly gross. Big companies that make potato chips know this as well, and they don't sell the same types of chips everywhere. They tailor the flavors to local tastes. You can find octopus chips in Japan, for example, and mushroom chips in Czechia (Czech Republic). Check out some of the strangest chip flavors from around the world.

CANADA
Maple syrup and moose meat (together as one flavor!)

CHINA
Blueberry (a best seller!)
Lemon tea
Hot and sour fish soup
Cucumber
Cola and chicken

CZECHIA
Mushroom

INDIA
Mint

JAPAN
Octopus
Salmon sushi

ROMANIA
Pickle

RUSSIA
Caviar (fish egg)

SOUTH AFRICA
Biltong (dried meat)

THAILAND
Squid

U.S.A.
Chocolate-covered chips
White chocolate and peppermint
Pecan pie

POTATO CHIP COMPANIES SOMETIMES HOLD CONTESTS FOR MEMBERS OF THE PUBLIC TO THINK UP NEW FLAVORS.

ICE CREAM TO MAKE YOU SCREAM

You might think of ice cream as a sweet dessert, but plenty of chefs and fancy ice-cream parlors have other ideas!

For example, how about some cheesy ice cream? You can have blue cheese ice cream served with a steak, or goat cheese and beetroot flavor as a starter. Or what about fish-flavored ice cream? An Australian restaurant created its own salmon and white chocolate ice cream, while in Los Angeles, U.S.A., you can try fish sauce ice cream. There's meat ice cream too, including flavors such as bacon, fig and turkey, and bone marrow (yes, bone marrow—the fatty stuff found in the middle of bones)! You can even get pizza, charcoal, or white chocolate banana curry flavored ice creams.

For the strangest flavors of all, try the ice cream parlors of Tokyo, Japan. Choose from cow tongue, squid ink, or octopus, or even raw horse meat ice cream. There's only one question left: Do you want a single scoop or a double?

DECISIONS, DECISIONS!

CREEPY-CRAWLY CHOCOLATE

There's nothing new about combining insects and chocolate. Chocolate-covered ants, for example, have been around for decades; they were first sold in the United States in the 1940s. But thanks to the modern trend of bingeing on bugs, chocolate makers are trying new recipes. You can now buy chocolate-dipped locusts, scorpions, and crickets, and boxes of superluxury chocolates, each topped with a crunchy bug sprinkled with edible gold dust. Fancy!

INSECT ICE CREAM

IN 2015, A MAGAZINE COMPANY HELD A CAMPAIGN TO ENCOURAGE PEOPLE TO THINK ABOUT THE BENEFITS OF EATING INSECTS. THEY SENT ICE-CREAM CARTS AROUND CITY STREETS TO HAND OUT FREE INSECT ICE CREAM. THE FLAVORS INCLUDED:

SCURRY BERRY: BERRY FLAVOR WITH CRUNCHY INSECT BITS

CHOC HOPPER: CHOCOLATE WITH GRASSHOPPERS

STRAWBERRIES AND SWIRLS: STRAWBERRY FLAVOR WITH MEALWORMS (A TYPE OF BEETLE LARVA)

AFTER ALL, BUGS ARE PREDICTED TO BECOME AN IMPORTANT FOOD FOR EVERYONE IN THE FUTURE. ENJOYING THEM COMBINED WITH ICE CREAM OR CHOCOLATE IS A TASTY WAY TO GET USED TO THE IDEA!

A BANANA SPLIT FEATURING FARM ANTS AND CRICKETS

TAIWAN'S FAMOUS MODERN TOILET CAFÉ (SEE PAGE 19) WILL SERVE YOU POOP ICE CREAM— BUT IT'S NOT ACTUALLY POOP FLAVORED. THANK GOODNESS FOR THAT! (IT'S CHOCOLATE, OF COURSE.)

A SCOOP OF "POOP"!

MEET THE MUMMIES!

EWW GROSS NASTY DISGUSTING

YUCK-O-METER

SEVERAL ANCIENT CULTURES PRESERVED DEAD BODIES, BUT THE ANCIENT EGYPTIANS ARE THE MOST FAMOUS OF ALL FOR TURNING THEIR DEAD VIPs INTO MUMMIES. Usually, when someone dies and is buried, their body rots, or decomposes, eventually ending up as little more than a spooky skeleton. But the Egyptians believed that you needed your whole body to have a good time in the afterlife.

Are You My MUMMY?

Egypt has a lot of desert, and early Egyptians simply buried their dead in the sand. It was so hot and dry that the bodies didn't rot, and they instead became naturally preserved mummies. However, wild animals could dig them up for a snack, and robbers could steal the personal possessions that people were buried with.

To prevent this, about 5,000 years ago, wealthy people began to bury their dead in coffins and tombs. But there was a disgusting downside: A coffin didn't preserve the body the way hot sand did, and soon the revolting rot would set in. So the Egyptians came up with another way to make sure the dead bodies couldn't decompose: mummification!

WHILE THE RICH WERE BURIED IN COFFINS, A PEASANT'S GRAVE WAS MORE LIKE THIS.

ONE EGYPTIAN NAMED URSU LEFT A CURSE THAT WARNS: "WHO SHALL INJURE MY TOMB OR DRAG OUT MY MUMMY ... HIS SOUL SHALL BE DESTROYED FOREVER." YIKES!

Macabre MUMMY-MAKING

Preparing a mummy was an extraordinarily gross process.

1. After giving the body a good wash, priests sliced it open and pulled out the lungs, liver, stomach, and guts. (These organs had to be mummified separately, or they could quickly cause the whole body to decompose.)

2. The embalmers left the heart where it was, as ancient Egyptians believed a person's mind, emotions, and personality were located there.

3. Next, they covered the body with natron, a type of salt, and left it for 70 days to soak up moisture and dry the body out. They did the same with the stomach and other organs.

4. The salt was removed, and the dried, leathery-skinned body was rubbed with oil. If the body was looking a little hollow, the embalmers stuffed the gaps with sawdust or cloth. They then wrapped the body in strips of linen cloth before laying it in its decorated coffin.

5. They put the organs into four jars with head-shaped lids, to be buried with the body. That way, the dead person could keep their organs, but they could be properly preserved too. The heads on the jars represented different gods who would watch over each organ.

EGYPTIAN JARS FOR HOLDING MUMMIFIED ORGANS, TODAY KNOWN AS CANOPIC JARS

ANUBIS, THE JACKAL-HEADED GOD OF THE DEAD, WAS BELIEVED TO GUIDE THE MUMMY-MAKING PROCESS.

A HOOK LIKE THIS WAS USED TO DRAW THE BRAIN OUT THROUGH THE NOSTRILS.

You Won't Be NEEDING THIS!

The ancient Egyptians didn't think the brain—unlike the heart—was all that important. It was also very soggy, making it hard to preserve. So instead of saving it, they threw it away. They stuck a long hook up the future mummy's nose to break up the brain and then scooped out the mashed pieces. What a headache!

THE MUMMY'S CURSE

MUMMIFICATION WORKED SO WELL THAT THE PRESERVED BODIES OF ANCIENT EGYPTIANS ARE STILL BEING FOUND TODAY, THOUSANDS OF YEARS LATER. THEY REVEAL A LOT ABOUT ANCIENT EGYPTIAN LIFE AND CULTURE. FOR EXAMPLE, THE TOMB AND MUMMY OF THE YOUNG PHARAOH TUTANKHAMUN, DISCOVERED IN 1922, HELPED HISTORIANS UNDERSTAND MORE ABOUT HIS LIFE AND TIME PERIOD.

BUT WOULD YOU WANT YOUR PRECIOUS TOMB TO BE DUG UP AND YOUR BODY UNWRAPPED LONG AFTER YOU DIED? SOME PEOPLE THINK DEAD BODIES SHOULD BE LEFT TO REST IN PEACE, INCLUDING THOSE OF AMAZING ANCIENT MUMMIES. AND THE ANCIENT EGYPTIANS THOUGHT SO TOO! SOME OF THEIR TOMBS HAVE INSCRIPTIONS ON THEIR WALLS, CURSING ANYONE WHO DARES TO DISTURB THEM. WHEN ARCHAEOLOGIST HOWARD CARTER UNEARTHED TUTANKHAMUN'S TOMB IN 1922, SOME PEOPLE BELIEVED A CURSE KILLED SEVERAL OF THE PEOPLE INVOLVED! HOWEVER, CARTER HIMSELF SURVIVED, SUGGESTING THAT CURSES HAD LITTLE TO DO WITH IT.

MUMMIES WERE OFTEN BURIED WITH FOOD—LIKE THIS DRIED BEEF—SO THEY WOULDN'T GET HUNGRY IN THE AFTERLIFE.

WRETCHED RODENTS

YUCK-O-METER
EWW · GROSS · NASTY · DISGUSTING

DOES THE THOUGHT OF SKITTERING LITTLE PAWS MAKE YOU CRINGE? And does the idea of a long, pink, wormlike tail make you want to jump and scream? For many people, the thought of finding a scampering, squeaking rat in their home is the height of horror. But why? What is really so scary about this cute, fluffy, beady-eyed bundle?

RATTY RUMORS

You've probably heard all kinds of scary things about rats. Check out these popular rumors to the right. Not all of these claims are true ... but some are!

For example, rats do dribble pee all the time. The smell of their own urine on the ground shows rats where they've been before, helping them to find their way. They pee on each other too, to show friendliness. And they even pee on food to show each other where there's something good to eat! (But don't take that tip from rats—your friends definitely wouldn't like that.) Read on to find out which of these other rumors are also true!

> Rats leave a trail of pee wherever they go!

> They can hold their breath and swim up out of your toilet!

> They gang up on people and eat them alive!

> They can squeeze through a hole the size of a quarter!

SOME PEOPLE LOVE RATS AND KEEP THEM AS PETS. SO THEY CAN'T BE THAT BAD ... CAN THEY?

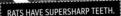

RATS HAVE SUPERSHARP TEETH.

PEOPLE EAT RATS TOO. THEY'RE A POPULAR SNACK IN VIETNAM, MYANMAR, NIGERIA, AND SEVERAL OTHER COUNTRIES. IN THE PAST, PEOPLE WHO RAN OUT OF FOOD WOULD OFTEN TURN TO ROASTING ANY RATS THEY COULD FIND TO KEEP THEMSELVES ALIVE.

RAT RATIONS

OK—so rats are pretty gross. But are they really all that scary? After all, they're cute, fuzzy mammals. The answer? Maybe ... because rats will eat just about ANYTHING.

RAT FAVORITES
Rats are very happy if there's a supply of grain, nuts, eggs, meat, fish, or yummy leftover human food such as pizza, pasta, or candy.

OK, THIS'LL HAVE TO DO
If their favorite foods aren't around, rats will munch on fruit, pet food, insects, snails, and household goods like leather and candles.

I'M STARVING!
Hungry rats aren't fussy. At all! They'll eat compost; rotten garbage; dog, cat, or horse poop; and their own poop. They'll also eat the bodies of other dead rats.

MMMMMMM, HUMAN FLESH!
Rats have been known to bite humans, especially at night. Some experts think that once a rat has bitten someone, it gets a taste for human blood and is more likely to bite again! However, rats don't normally devour a whole human ... but it could technically happen. If someone were very weak or couldn't move, and there were lots of hungry rats around, that person could get eaten. Yikes! Of course, it's not at all likely.

OM NOM NOM!

EASY PEASY, RAT SQUEEZY

Rats really can squeeze through tiny spaces. An average-size rat can get through a hole just one inch (2.5 cm) wide (about the size of a quarter) by flattening its rib cage. Rats can also hold their breath underwater. That means that a rat—if it was really determined—could swim up from a sewer, wriggle through narrow pipes, and jump out of a toilet! Most rats wouldn't bother, though, when there's a sewer full of tasty poop to munch.

DEADLY DISEASES

However, there's another reason why rats are disgustingly dangerous—they spread deadly diseases. They hang out in garbage, sewers, and poop, so they're covered in germs. Rat bites, droppings, and pee can give us horrible diseases like typhus, meningitis, and rat-bite fever. Not to mention that the bubonic plague, or Black Death, which killed millions of people in the Middle Ages, might have been spread by fleas living on rats.

RATS CAN FIT INTO TINY PLACES.

FOUL FESTIVALS

GROSS · NASTY · EWW · DISGUSTING

YUCK-O-METER

IF YOU'RE READING THIS BOOK, YOU PROBABLY THINK THAT GROSS STUFF CAN BE TONS OF FUN. And luckily for you, you're not alone! Thousands of people around the world love to flock to festivals that celebrate the disgusting, the smelly, and the super weird. Check out these truly yucky—and we mean that in a good way—events!

MOOSE POOP GALORE!

PARTY POOPERS

THE VILLAGE OF TALKEETNA, ALASKA, U.S.A., WAS SO PROUD OF ITS LOCAL MOOSE POPULATION, IT DECIDED TO SET UP ITS OWN SPECIAL CELEBRATION OF MOOSE DROPPINGS (POOP, THAT IS!). The Moose Dropping Festival ran every year for 37 years, from 1972 to 2009. The star attraction was the Moose Dropping Raffle, a game of chance with simple rules.

Hundreds of pieces of moose poop were collected, dried, labeled with numbers, and sold like raffle tickets. They were then put into a sack and hoisted high above a target painted on the ground. The bag was opened—and the poop went flying! The numbered nugget that ended up closest to the target won its owner a cash prize.

Besides the raffle, there were contests to throw moose droppings at a target board, and stalls selling jewelry, key rings, and ornaments made from dried-out moose poop. Now, that's a big to-do about doo-doo!

FAR-FLUNG DUNG

A COMPETITOR CATCHES A COW CHIP.

SADLY, THE MOOSE DROPPING FESTIVAL IS NO MORE. BECAUSE IT BECAME SO POPULAR AND OVERCROWDED, THE VILLAGE VOTED TO STOP HOLDING IT. But don't panic! You can still take part in poop-related pursuits at the Wisconsin State Cow Chip Throw and Festival. During the festival, which is held in Prairie du Sac, Wisconsin, U.S.A., every September, competitors see who can fling cow feces the farthest!

Cow Chip Throw competitors take the contest super seriously, carefully selecting the best cow chips before hurling them across a field. Competitors aren't allowed to wear gloves, but they are allowed to lick their hands to get a better grip. And the record for the farthest-flung cow poop is at least 248 feet (76 m). Just don't get in the way!

> COW CHIP THROWING IS STRANGELY SIMILAR TO THE OLYMPIC SPORT OF DISCUS THROWING, WHICH DATES FROM ANCIENT GREEK TIMES.

FOOD FIGHT FRENZY

IN 1945, A SUMMER PARADE IN THE SMALL TOWN OF BUÑOL, SPAIN, TURNED MESSY WHEN A PERFORMER WAS ACCIDENTALLY PUSHED OVER. In a rage, he grabbed handfuls of tomatoes from a nearby stall and began throwing them around. People who were splatted by them threw more back, and suddenly—tomato fight!

The fight was so much fun that some of the locals decided to do it again the next year. At first, the town cracked down and banned the messy tomato mush-fest, but eventually, they agreed to make it an official event. Every August, the festival, called La Tomatina, attracts thousands of tourists from all over the world. In fact, they have to sell tickets to limit the tomato fighters to just 20,000 people to make it safer!

On the day itself, trucks deliver 150 tons (136 t) of ripe tomatoes to the town square. Once a starter gun kicks off the fight, participants throw tomatoes at each other for about two hours. Of course, there are strict rules: People are allowed to throw only tomatoes, and the tomatoes must be squashed before being flung. Still, it's not for the faint of heart—players wear goggles to protect their eyes from stinging tomato juice, and extra-grip shoes so they don't slip on the slush-covered sidewalks.

Afterward, the square is covered in so many squashed tomatoes, it needs to be hosed down by fire trucks. Smaller hoses are used to wash down the players!

A GURNING CHAMPION CELEBRATES HIS WIN.

THAT'S JUST WEIRD!

ENGLAND HAS WHAT MIGHT BE THE WORLD'S WEIRDEST LOCAL CONTESTS. YOU CAN TRY …

TOE WRESTLING, DERBYSHIRE
LIKE ARM WRESTLING OR THUMB WRESTLING, BUT WITH TOES! OPPONENTS MUST PUSH EACH OTHER'S TOES SIDEWAYS TO WIN. BEFORE BEING ALLOWED TO PLAY, THEY HAVE THEIR FEET CHECKED FOR AILMENTS LIKE ATHLETE'S FOOT OR WARTS.

WORM CHARMING, DEVON
AT THE ANNUAL WORM CHARMING CHAMPIONSHIPS, CONTESTANTS COAX AS MANY EARTHWORMS AS THEY CAN OUT OF A SMALL PATCH OF SOIL.

GURNING, CUMBRIA
GURNING MEANS MAKING WEIRD FACES! THIS BIZARRE FACE-PULLING CONTEST IS PART OF THE EGREMONT CRAB FAIR, A FESTIVAL THAT DATES BACK 750 YEARS.

STINKY, SICKLY SHIPS

YOU MAY HAVE HEARD THAT OLD SAILING SHIPS HAD A "POOP DECK." BUT THIS HAD NOTHING TO DO WITH POOP! WHILE POOPING HAPPENED AT THE VERY FRONT OF THE SHIP, THE POOP DECK WAS A HIGH-LEVEL DECK AT THE BACK END, OR STERN.

NASTY
GROSS
DISGUSTING
EWW
YUCK-O-METER

HUNDREDS OF YEARS AGO, THERE WAS ONLY ONE WAY TO TRAVEL ACROSS THE SEA: on a smelly, slow, creaky, dangerous, rat-infested sailing ship. Using the wind to blow them to and fro, sailing ships carried cargo, explorers, passengers, and pirates around the world. On journeys that took weeks or months, everyone was squashed together in a cramped space riddled with rats, germs, and creepy-crawlies, with food and water supplies growing more rank and rotten by the day. Could you have coped with life on board?

SMELLY SAILORS

In the past, a sailing ship had no showers, baths, or sinks. In fact, the crew couldn't wash for the entire journey, as the water on board was too precious to use for anything but drinking. Sailors didn't wash their clothes, either; they just kept the same outfit on nonstop, so they were often crawling with body lice. As you can imagine, bedding down for the night in a cabin full of sweaty, unwashed, lice-ridden crewmates smelled pretty bad.

On old wooden sailing ships, if you needed to poop, you went to the "head" at the bow (or front) of the ship. It had two holes, one on each side, to act as toilets. The waste fell into the water, and the ocean spray splashing the front of the ship kept it clean.

Unfortunately, sailors didn't always make it to the head, especially during a storm. Urine often ended up on the floorboards instead, and it dripped down into the bottom of the ship, along with vomit from anyone who was seasick, and—wait for it—diarrhea from sailors who had caught stomach diseases such as dysentery. It all collected in the bottom of the ship's hull, called the bilge, where it swilled about with water that had leaked into the ship.

This filthy mixture, called bilge water, made the whole ship stink. Sailors had to take turns going down into the hull with buckets to bail the revolting bilge out.

A SHIP'S "HEAD"

WEEVILS FEAST ON SHIP RATIONS.

WHAT'S FOR LUNCH?

At least you could relieve the monotony of a slow sea journey with a delicious meal. Just kidding! Food on board sailing ships was notoriously revolting. Here's what a typical sailor might get to eat ...

🍀 Salted meat—usually beef or pork, dried and salted in barrels to preserve it, which made it very hard and chewy. Despite this, it still went rotten. The ships' cooks boiled it up into a greasy stew to make it a bit softer.

🍀 Hardtack, or ship's biscuit—rock-hard slabs made from flour and water. As the journey went on, the hardtack would be invaded by insects called weevils. The weevils' eggs later hatched into maggots. To make matters worse, the hardtack was often nibbled and peed on by the ships' rats too.

🍀 Ships also carried a type of very hard cheese (are you sensing a theme here?). It was so hard, sailors sometimes carved it into useful objects like buttons, instead of eating it. But someone did like it: Wriggly cheese worms would start living in it after a while.

POOP DECK

HEAD

BILGE

DEADLY DISEASE ON THE HIGH SEAS

IF YOU THINK EATING THE DISGUSTING DIET DESCRIBED HERE MIGHT MAKE YOU ILL, YOU'D BE RIGHT. WHEN SAILING SHIPS BEGAN MAKING LONGER JOURNEYS, TO EXPLORE DISTANT LANDS ACROSS THE OCEANS, SAILORS BEGAN DYING FROM A TERRIBLE DISEASE. THEY BECAME EXHAUSTED, WEAK, AND DEPRESSED. THEIR SKIN WAS COVERED IN BRUISE-LIKE MARKS AND BLEEDING BLISTERS. THEIR RIBS COULD BE HEARD RATTLING IN THEIR CHESTS. THEIR GUMS BEGAN TO ROT AND RECEDE, THEIR TEETH FELL OUT, AND THEY HAD TERRIBLE-SMELLING BREATH. IF THEY DIDN'T RETURN TO SHORE SOON, THEY DIED.

AT FIRST, NO ONE KNEW WHAT CAUSED THIS HORRIFIC SICKNESS. BUT IN THE 1700S, SCIENTISTS DISCOVERED IT WAS CAUSED BY A LACK OF FRESH FRUIT AND VEGETABLES (AS THE BODY NEEDS THE VITAMIN C THEY PROVIDE). THE PROBLEM WAS SOLVED WHEN SHIPS BEGAN TAKING SUPPLIES OF CITRUS FRUITS AND PICKLED CABBAGE ON THEIR VOYAGES.

WITHOUT ENOUGH VITAMIN C, PEOPLE COULD GET SCURVY AND END UP LIKE THIS. NOW YOU KNOW WHY YOU NEED TO EAT YOUR FRUITS AND VEGGIES!

NASTY NAILS

LOOK AT THE ENDS OF YOUR FINGERS, OR YOUR TOES. Check out those claws! No—really! Fingernails and toenails are the human version of animals' claws and hooves. They are made of keratin, the same substance that makes up many animal horns, hooves, and shells. Nails can be useful for many things, including scratching your head, peeling off stickers, or opening envelopes. But they can also be extremely gross—especially underneath.

IF YOU HAVE ONUXOPHOBIA, YOU PROBABLY WON'T BE READING THIS! IT'S A PHOBIA OF NAILS, ESPECIALLY TOUCHING THEM, OR HAVING YOURS TOUCHED (OR EVEN WORSE, TRIMMED!).

WHAT LURKS BENEATH

IF YOU DON'T MAKE AN EFFORT TO KEEP YOUR NAILS CLEAN, THEY COULD END UP LIKE THIS!

Even when you think your nails are scrubbed perfectly clean, they're not. The gap underneath the tip of a toenail or fingernail (called the subungual area) is the perfect place for dirt to get stuck, and for germs and other gross gunk to hide. A typical nail is normally home to hundreds of thousands of germs. Take a look at this close-up photo of a dirty fingernail, and you'll see why you're not supposed to leave clipped nails lying around!

Fingernails can harbor dangerous germs, like salmonella, which causes food poisoning. Not to mention other really gross things like parasitic worm eggs (see page 68) and tiny skin creepy-crawlies such as mites. That's why people wear disposable gloves to prepare food in factories or to carry out surgery.

Scientists have found that people with artificial or very long nails have extra germs under them. However, as long as your nails are short, neat, and well washed, wearing nail polish does not make germs worse.

STOP NIBBLING THOSE NAILS

OUCH OUCH OUCH!

Nail-biting is the most common nervous habit in the world. Though it may not be as disgustingly rude as nose-picking or spitting, there's a reason why people tell you not to do it. *Lots* of reasons, in fact!

- Obviously, when your nails go in your mouth, so do all those germs, potential worm eggs, and other filth. Ew.

- Making your nails wet with slobber makes them even more attractive to germs, which love warm, damp places.

- In fact, too much saliva on your fingertips will start to digest (that is, EAT) and break down your skin, making it sore.

- It can even break your teeth! Some hardened fingernail biters end up with chipped or cracked teeth.

- If you bite too far, the sensitive nail bed is exposed. Sometimes, this can even make your nails stop growing.

- And if you SWALLOW a bitten-off nail, it can get stuck in your throat, which means a trip to the emergency room to have it picked out with long tweezers.

But don't panic! The occasional sneaky nibble probably won't do you too much harm—as long as you've washed your hands.

NAIL FAILS

Nails may be handy, but they can encounter all kinds of problems. Toenails attacked by a fungus can turn yellow, thick, and scaly. Big toenails sometimes become "ingrown," meaning the nail grows sideways and digs into the toe flesh. It's horribly painful, and in worst-case scenarios can result in having to have the whole toenail pulled out!

If you've ever been unlucky enough to slam a door on your fingernail, or hit it with a hammer, you might have had it fall off by itself after turning black all over. Nails that fall off do slowly grow back. Unless, that is, a doctor needs to remove someone's pesky, troublesome toenail once and for all. In that case, they can banish it permanently by also removing the nail bed.

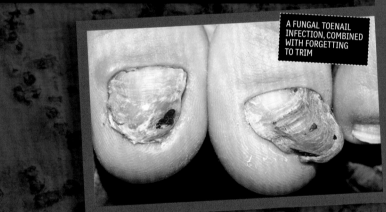

A FUNGAL TOENAIL INFECTION, COMBINED WITH FORGETTING TO TRIM

NAILED IT!

ONE VERY TIME-CONSUMING WAY TO BAG YOURSELF A WORLD RECORD IS TO GROW YOUR FINGERNAILS AS LONG AS POSSIBLE. HOW LONG CAN THEY GROW? WELL, INDIAN RECORD-HOLDER SHRIDHAR CHILLAL'S THUMBNAIL MEASURED ALMOST 6.5 FEET (2 M) LONG! AS NAILS GROW, THEY USUALLY CURL OVER OR EVEN FORM A COIL. OF COURSE, HAVING RECORD-BREAKING NAILS MAKES EVERYDAY TASKS PRETTY DIFFICULT. THERE ARE RECORDS FOR LONGEST NAILS ON BOTH HANDS, OR JUST ON A SINGLE HAND— THE EASIER OPTION!

SHRIDHAR CHILLAL OF INDIA HOLDS THE RECORD FOR LONGEST NAILS EVER ON A SINGLE HAND.

A CHAJCHAS IS A SOUTH AMERICAN PERCUSSION INSTRUMENT, MADE FROM GOAT OR LLAMA TOENAILS.

NATURE'S
MESSIEST MUNCHERS

DO YOU KNOW ANYONE WITH LESS-THAN-PERFECT TABLE MANNERS? Do they slurp their soup, chew with their mouth open, or let out a big belch at the table? Well, it could be worse. A lot worse. Just be grateful you don't have to sit next to any of these abominable animals while they're chowing down.

GROSS NASTY DISGUSTING EWW

YUCK-O-METER

EXCUSE YOU!

As everyone knows, if the food you want is far away at the other end of the table, you politely say, "Please pass the potatoes!" But wouldn't it be easier if you could shoot out a huge sticky tongue, like a chameleon does, and simply grab yourself a mouthful? A chameleon's tongue can be as long as its whole body, or even longer, and it's covered in super-sticky mucus.

The tongue shoots out in a split second, and its funnel-shaped tip plops right onto the prey, which has no chance to escape. Then the tongue retracts and hauls the wriggling morsel back into the chameleon's mouth.

A CHAMELEON USES ITS TONGUE TO NAB LUNCH.

DRACULA ANTS GET THEIR NAME BECAUSE THEY SUCK BLOOD FROM THEIR OWN BABIES! THEY BITE HOLES IN THE LARVAE AND HELP THEMSELVES TO A DRINK.

A LARGE PYTHON ABOUT TO SWALLOW A KANGAROO

MASSIVE MEAL

It's probably best to avoid eating so much that you can't walk, or even get up. Still, if you're a snake, it's only natural!

All snakes are meat-eaters. While some use venomous bites to kill prey, others, known as constrictors, squeeze their lunch to death by coiling their bodies tightly around it. The biggest constrictors, such as the anaconda and the reticulated python, are the most likely to try gulping down really enormous prey. We're talking kangaroos, cows, and even full-size crocodiles.

Unsurprisingly, after a lunch like that, a snake is ready for a nap. In fact, it has no choice, because it can't move! The snake has to lie around with a huge lump in its body until its stomach juices have slowly dissolved and digested the prey.

A SNAKE'S JAWS ARE HELD TOGETHER BY LOOSE, STRETCHY LIGAMENTS, LIKE ELASTIC BANDS. IT CAN PULL ITS JAWBONES AWAY FROM EACH OTHER TO STRETCH ITS MOUTH WIDE OPEN.

GINORMOUS GULPERS

The black swallower is a deep-sea fish with an amazing appetite. It's happy to gulp down other fish up to twice its own length, and 10 times its own weight! How? The swallower has an incredibly stretchy stomach that expands and hangs down below its body when it's full of a monster meal. The fish gets so stretched, its stomach becomes transparent, and you can see what's inside. Even grosser, sometimes the sagging stomachful of food takes so long to digest, it starts to rot and release gases. These make the fish float up to the sea surface, where it dies.

BLACK SWALLOWER

AND THE WINNER IS ...

WHEN IT COMES TO DISGUSTING DINING BEHAVIOR, THERE'S ONE ANIMAL THAT BEATS ALL THE REST CLAWS DOWN. IT'S THE WELL AND TRULY REVOLTING KOMODO DRAGON. THIS GIANT LIZARD HAS A VAST RANGE OF VILE HABITS, INCLUDING:

🔔 TEARING HUGE CHUNKS OUT OF DYING PREY, AND GOBBLING THEM DOWN AT HIGH SPEED.

🔔 GULPING SMALLER PREY WHOLE, AND SOMETIMES RAMMING IT AGAINST A TREE TO HELP PUSH IT DOWN.

🔔 DROOLING HUGE AMOUNTS OF SLIPPERY SALIVA TO HELP ITS MASSIVE MOUTHFULS SLIDE DOWN MORE EASILY.

🔔 VOMITING TO OFF-LOAD EXTRA WEIGHT, SO IT CAN RUN AWAY IF IN DANGER.

🔔 TAKING UP TO 20 MINUTES TO SWALLOW A GOAT. (THE DRAGON HAS A HANDY TUBE UNDER ITS TONGUE, SO IT CAN BREATHE AT THE SAME TIME.)

🔔 COUGHING UP A HUGE, SLIMY, STINKY LUMP OF ANIMAL FUR, HORNS, AND BONES AFTER EATING, KNOWN AS A GASTRIC PELLET.

🔔 DIGGING UP HUMAN GRAVES TO SNACK ON THE CONTENTS!

TOADSTOOLS OF TERROR

NASTY
DISGUSTING
...-METER

YOU'RE TAKING A WALK IN THE WOODS, PERHAPS GAZING UP AT THE TREES AND BIRDS, WHEN—SQUELCH! You stumble over something slippery, clammy, and truly horrifying. Slimy, stinky, and sometimes deadly poisonous, toadstools and mushrooms aren't plants, but belong to the fungi family. While some may have a familiar mushroom shape, others can resemble a dead human hand, someone's severed ear, or a tentacled alien from outer space! Check out our guide to some of the most ...earsome and freaky fungi on the planet.

WITCHES' BUTTER

: *Exidia glandulosa*
...mp is 1 to 2 inches (2.5 to 5 cm) across
...dead tree branches, in cool northern areas

...oking fungus gets its name from its squishy,
...re. If witches did exist, they might like to
...dead trees to spread on their toast. It grows
...napes that clump together to form a black,
...

BLEEDING TOOTH
FUNGUS

LATIN NAME: *Hydnellum peckii*
SIZE: Up to 8 inches (20 cm) across
SPOTTED: In conifer forests in North America, Europe, and Asia

If you thought you couldn't really get grossed out by a toadstool, this is the frightful fungus to change your mind! As it grows, the velvety white fungus leaks out drops of a gruesome, bright red, blood-like liquid.

STARFISH **STINKHORN**

LATIN NAME: *Aseroe rubra*
SIZE: 4 inches (10 cm) across
SPOTTED: Gardens and grassy areas in Australia and Oceania

Although it's known as the starfish stinkhorn or the sea anemone fungus, this many-tentacled toadstool's Latin name really translates to "disgusting red" fungus. On top of a thick pink stalk, it sprouts between 6 and 10 bright red tentacles, with a large blob of brownish grey slime in the middle.

STINKHORN SPORES ARE STORED IN A STICKY GOOP CALLED THE GLEBA, WHICH IS IRRESISTIBLE TO FLIES.

DEAD MAN'S FINGERS

LATIN NAME: *Xylaria polymorpha*
SIZE: Up to 4 inches (10 cm) tall
SPOTTED: Woodlands in North America and Europe

As this terrifying toadstool sprouts out of the ground, it looks like the fingers of a decaying zombie trying to escape from its grave. Not only are the "fingers" a ghoulish gray-blue color, they also come complete with deathly pale fingernails!

SMELLY **STINKHORNS**

AS IF THEY DON'T LOOK DISGUSTING ENOUGH, SOME TOADSTOOLS CAN ALSO SMELL REALLY BAD—ESPECIALLY THE FAMILY OF FUNGI KNOWN AS STINKHORNS. THEY RELEASE THE STENCH OF ANIMAL POOP OR DEAD, ROTTING BODIES IN ORDER TO ATTRACT FLIES. A BIT LIKE BEES POLLINATING FLOWERS, THE FLIES BECOME COVERED IN THE STINKHORN'S STICKY SPORES (FUNGUS SEEDS) AND HELP TO SPREAD THEM TO OTHER AREAS TO START GROWING.

THE DISGUSTING RED FUNGUS IS A STINKHORN, AND SO IS A TOADSTOOL CALLED THE "STINKY SQUID." BESIDES SMELLING LIKE PIG POOP, THIS FUNGUS ALSO HAPPENS TO RESEMBLE AN ALIEN CLAW AS IT EMERGES FROM THE SOIL.

JELLY EAR

LATIN NAME: *Auricularia auricula-judae*
SIZE: Up to 4 inches (10 cm) across
SPOTTED: Growing on trees in most parts of the world

Be careful what you say in the forest—the trees have ears! The "jelly ear" fungus can look exactly like a human ear, but it's a real toadstool that grows on tree trunks and logs. Some have veinlike parts and fuzzy hairs, making them even more realistic!

BRAIN **FUNGUS**

LATIN NAME: *Gyromitra esculenta*
SIZE: Up to 6 inches (15 cm) across
SPOTTED: Forest floors in North America and Europe

To add to the creepy collection of Halloween props on this page, this fungus looks just like a life-size, reddish, wrinkled human brain, growing on its own white brain stem. It can also be horribly poisonous.

QUIZ
NAME THAT SLIMY STUFF!

BY NOW YOU'VE SEEN SO MUCH REVOLTING AND YUCKY STUFF, YOU SHOULD BE GETTING PRETTY GOOD AT TELLING SLIME, SNOT, AND SALIVA APART FROM POOP, VOMIT, AND MONSTROUS PARASITES ... OR ARE YOU? Well, one way to find out for sure is to take this truly disgusting picture test. Simply study each photo closely, then decide what the gross gunk, object, or creature could possibly be!

3 WHICH ANIMAL LEFT BEHIND THESE CRAZY CUBE-SHAPED DROPPINGS?

A. A domestic goat

B. A Chinese pangolin

C. The rare and little-known square-ended duck

D. A common wombat

1 UGH, WHAT'S THIS WEIRD YELLOW STUFF?

A. A type of slime mold known as "dog vomit"

B. Actual dog vomit

C. Spilled scrambled eggs

D. Toad poop

4 OH NO—*WHAT* IS THIS HORRIFYING LUMPY GREEN STUFF?

A. The insides of a frog that were spit out by a heron

B. A type of bacteria that turns into jelly when it's wet

C. A sample of slime collected from the surface of Mars

D. A ginormous booger sneezed out by a blue whale

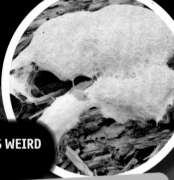

2 WHO IS POSING FOR THE CAMERA IN THIS CHARMING CLOSE-UP?

A. A deep-sea bobbit worm

B. A hawk moth caterpillar

C. A bluebottle fly maggot

D. A pork tapeworm

5 YOU CAN SOMETIMES FIND THIS ON THE BEACH ... BUT WHAT IS IT?

A. An animal called a black sea hare

B. A lump of sticky oil leaked from a tanker ship

C. A large shark's egg case

D. A type of slimy, jellylike seaweed

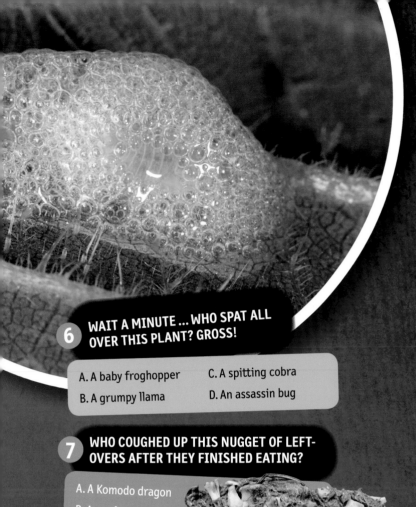

6 WAIT A MINUTE ... WHO SPAT ALL OVER THIS PLANT? GROSS!

A. A baby froghopper

B. A grumpy llama

C. A spitting cobra

D. An assassin bug

7 WHO COUGHED UP THIS NUGGET OF LEFT-OVERS AFTER THEY FINISHED EATING?

A. A Komodo dragon

B. An owl

C. A garter snake

D. A carrion crow

8 WHAT ON EARTH IS THIS CREEPY BRIGHT GREEN THING, SPOTTED ON A TAIWANESE DOCKSIDE?

A. A previously unknown species that scientists named the slime snake

B. A severed octopus tentacle that fell off a fishing boat

C. A glowing poop left by a seal that had been eating bioluminescent algae

D. A marine ribbon worm, which usually lives in the sea

9 JUST WHAT *IS* THAT THING HANGING OUT OF THAT SHARK'S MOUTH?

A. It's the shark's swollen tongue after it was stung by a jellyfish.

B. It's all that's left of a rotten octopus.

C. It's the shark's own stomach, which it just turned inside out and vomited up.

D. It's a whale brain, one of the shark's favorite snacks.

ANSWERS:

1. A) A TYPE OF SLIME MOLD KNOWN AS "DOG VOMIT"
Slime molds are weird fungus-like creatures that can creep and crawl around.

2. C) A BLUEBOTTLE FLY MAGGOT
Now you know what maggots' faces look like.

3. D) A COMMON WOMBAT
Strange but true—wombats poop cubes. There's no such thing as a square-ended duck.

4. B) A TYPE OF BACTERIA THAT TURNS INTO JELLY WHEN IT'S WET
This bacteria, called Nostoc, is found in soil and water or on rocks.

5. A) AN ANIMAL CALLED A BLACK SEA HARE
It's a VERY big species of sea slug.

6. A) A BABY FROGHOPPER
This baby insect makes itself a protective covering by squirting liquid out of its butt, then blowing bubbles into it.

7. B) AN OWL
Owls cough up pellets of bones, claws, and fur after eating their prey whole. Crows and Komodo dragons do too, but their pellets look different.

8. D) A MARINE RIBBON WORM, WHICH USUALLY LIVES IN THE SEA
We rarely see these water worms, but they come in many colors and can grow to over 100 feet (30.5 m) long.

9. C) IT'S THE SHARK'S OWN STOMACH, WHICH IT JUST TURNED INSIDE OUT AND VOMITED UP.
Some sharks, rays, frogs, and toads do this to clean their stomachs out.

HOW DID YOU DO?

1–3 CORRECT ANSWERS
Oh dear. You're a little clueless about gross stuff—but this book is here to help!

4–6 CORRECT ANSWERS
Not bad! You're well on the way to becoming a great gross gunk identifier.

7–9 CORRECT ANSWERS
Excellent. You know gross and disgusting substances like the back of your hand. *Eww*—what is that on the back of your hand?!

FOUL FASHION

NASTY

GROSS

DISGUSTING

EWW

YUCK-O-METER

OH MY, DO WE SPOT SOME HAUTE COUTURE? Fashion is all about expressing yourself and making a statement. And what better way to surprise and shock than to wear clothes made of something gross, creepy, or even creepy-crawly? Step this way to explore the freakier fringes of fashion!

STEAK
STYLE STATEMENT

DON'T TRY THIS AT HOME!

In 2010, pop star Lady Gaga made headlines around the globe when she wore a dress made of raw meat. Designer Franc Fernandez had made the dress to order just before the event, using uncooked pieces of beef flank steak, so that it would still be fresh on the night.

You wouldn't expect a meat dress to last long, especially under sweltering hot stage lights. And sure enough, it did begin to go bad soon afterward. It was quickly put into a freezer to stop the rot. Eventually, to preserve the dress long-term, a taxidermist stepped in. He thawed the dress out (which meant it soon started to smell stinky) and treated the meat with germ-killing chemicals. The meat "fabric" ended up much harder and tougher than it was to start with, a little like beef jerky. But the taxidermist still managed to mount it on a mannequin, and it was put on display at the Rock & Roll Hall of Fame in Cleveland, Ohio, U.S.A.

LADY GAGA'S FULL OUTFIT ALSO INCLUDED A MATCHING MEAT HAT, PURSE, AND BOOTS. SHE DESCRIBED THE OUTFIT AS FEELING VERY CHILLY TO WEAR!

A FASHION FIRST?

Although it amazed the world, Lady Gaga's was not the first ever meat dress. Years before, British artist and singer Linder Sterling performed on stage with her band while wearing a dress made of leftover chicken meat from a restaurant. Six months prior to that, activist Ann Simonton went on a protest march wearing a dress made of slices of bologna sausage and carrying a sign that read "Judge Meat Not Women." Simonton also wore a hot dog sausage necklace to match (she ended up being followed down the street by hungry stray dogs). She later donated the dress to dogs when she was done wearing it!

GLITTERING BUG BALL GOWN

Dresses made of ... *unusual* ... materials are nothing new. Over 100 years ago, a famous theater star named Ellen Terry had her own freaky frock moment. She dazzled audiences by wearing a full-length green robe adorned with the wings of 1,000 iridescent beetles! The beetles' hard, shiny wing cases were dried out and didn't rot away, and the dress was later restored and put on display.

THE BEETLE WING DRESS BECAME ALMOST AS FAMOUS AS TERRY HERSELF.

FABRICS OF THE FUTURE

INVENTORS, SCIENTISTS, AND ARTISTS ARE EXPERIMENTING WITH NEW WAYS TO MAKE FABRICS AND CLOTHES USING LIVING THINGS. THEY COULD ONE DAY BE USED AS NATURAL, BIODEGRADABLE ALTERNATIVES TO SYNTHETIC FABRICS, WHICH CAN CONTRIBUTE TO POLLUTION.

BACTERIA FABRIC FACTORY
DESIGNER SUZANNE LEE HAS DEVELOPED A WAY TO MAKE LEATHERLIKE FABRIC BY USING VATS OF BACTERIA TO MAKE GLOOPY MATS OF A NATURAL SUBSTANCE CALLED CELLULOSE. THIS CAN THEN BE SHAPED INTO CLOTHES AND SHOES—BUT IT DOES DISSOLVE BACK INTO SLIME IF IT GETS WET!

FECES FABRIC
CELLULOSE IS ALSO FOUND IN GRASS, AND IN COW POOP (WHICH IS MADE OF GRASS!). IT CAN BE COLLECTED FROM COW DUNG AND MADE INTO A TYPE OF NON-SMELLY POOP-BASED TEXTILE.

HAGFISH SLIME SILK
RESEARCHERS HAVE DRIED OUT THE STRINGY SLIME MADE BY DEEP-SEA HAGFISH (SEE PAGES 42–43) AND USED IT TO SPIN A FINE, SILKY THREAD.

IN VICTORIAN TIMES, IT WAS NORMAL TO MAKE RINGS AND OTHER JEWELRY FROM YOUR CHILD'S BABY TEETH.

STRANDS OF SALIVA

Silk is a well-known fabric, and it usually isn't considered weird or gross at all—in fact, it's seen as luxurious and glamorous. But it actually comes from a type of insect, the silk moth caterpillar. The caterpillar makes the silk using glands in its mouth that are similar to salivary glands, so you could almost say that silk is really caterpillar spit.

When the caterpillar has finished feeding and is ready to transform into an adult, it starts producing a long, single strand of silk, which it winds into a cocoon around itself. To make silk, silk farmers boil the completed cocoons and then unwind the thread. The caterpillars don't survive this, which is why vegans don't wear silk.

DRINKS THAT ARE HARD TO SWALLOW

GROSS NASTY DISGUSTING EWW

YUCK-O-METER

THIS BOOK IS SO FULL OF STOMACH-CHURNING CHOW, from maggot cheese to old rotting sharks to crispy fried spiders, that you're going to need something to wash it all down! This selection of drinks from around the world should do the trick.

CHEW SOME CHICHA

Head to Peru or Chile in South America, and you'll probably be offered *chicha*, a fermented corn drink. Sounds good—until you discover the traditional chicha-making method. When brewing a big vat of chicha, everyone gathers to chew great mouthfuls of corn ... and then spit the corn mush into a large container! Then, after the munched mush is boiled with water and spices, it's left to ferment for several weeks.

Most chicha these days is made without added saliva, but some people still use the old method to make their own chicha at home. And it's not just because they like the taste of days-old drool—there's actually a good reason for it. Saliva contains chemicals that break the corn down into sugar, which helps it to ferment.

DEPENDING ON THE TYPE OF CORN USED TO MAKE IT, CHICHA CAN BE YELLOW OR PURPLE.

THE BLOOD MILK IS SHARED ON SPECIAL OCCASIONS.

BLOOD BREW

Why bother with a complicated chewing process, though, when you could simply enjoy a pure, fresh cup of blood? It's natural, tasty, and full of protein! Many people find the idea of drinking blood gruesome, and they associate it with vampires from horror stories—but it's actually a common and useful practice around the world.

In Kenya, Africa, some cattle-farming people, such as the Maasai, make a drink of cows' blood mixed with milk. They take only a little blood at a time from their cows, making sure they're not killing them. This gives them some of the advantages of eating meat without having to lose their valuable animals.

In Vietnam, a glass of freshly squeezed snake blood is sometimes considered a health drink. People can buy it in restaurants or from street sellers. Besides supposedly giving you the vitality of a snake, the blood is said to bring good fortune and prosperity. (There's no actual evidence it works, though!)

And in the 13th century, when the horse-riding warriors of the Mongol Empire were on the rampage, they would stop and have a sip of their own horses' blood to keep them going!

PANDA POOP TEA

Fancy a cup of the world's most expensive tea? That would be panda poop tea. It's incredibly rare, because it's grown in piles of panda poop. And as pandas themselves are rare, their poop is too! Luckily, some industrious tea makers collect the dung from local panda rehabilitation centers and then grow the tea. A single cup of panda poop tea costs over $100—and it's said to taste "nutty." Well, at least it doesn't taste poopy!

STOMACH-CHURNING SODAS

WHAT'S THE WEIRDEST SODA FLAVOR YOU'VE EVER HAD? MIXED BERRY? A LIMITED-EDITION FLAVOR WITH A CRAZY NAME? WELL, HOW ABOUT BEEF? OR CHEESE? GET READY FOR SOME OF THE MOST NAUSEATING SODAS FROM AROUND THE WORLD!

JAPAN
- TERIYAKI BEEF
- KIMCHI (PICKLED CABBAGE)
- EEL

UNITED STATES
- TURKEY-AND-GRAVY
- CHEESY TORTILLA CHIP
- COLA-AND-YOGURT

CHINA
- BIRD'S NEST

A (PEE) DRINK A DAY KEEPS THE DOCTOR AWAY

In India, cow pee is sold as a health drink! It's known as "cow water" and is said to protect against all kinds of illnesses. Little bottles of the curious cure are sold in some stores alongside other cow products, like milk and yogurt.

BOTTLES OF "COW WATER"

HORRIBLE HUNTING HABITS

GROSS · NASTY · EWW · DISGUSTING

YUCK-O-METER

GRUESOME AS IT MAY SEEM, IT'S A FACT OF NATURE THAT ANIMALS EAT OTHER ANIMALS. But at least most of them have the decency to grab their unlucky lunch and gobble it up quickly. Others, like the creatures on these pages, have some absolutely disgusting ways of catching and devouring their prey.

Sticky Ropes OF DOOM

It's a creature straight from your nightmares—and that's before it's even started snacking! The velvet worm isn't a worm, but it gets its name because of its soft, velvety body. Unlike actual worms, it has lots of legs (up to 86 of them!), each tipped with two sharp claws; two large, squishy antennae; and two slime-squirting tubes.

This creepy critter hunts at night, moving slowly and silently, using its antennae to sniff out something to eat. When it gets close, the velvet worm suddenly squirts two "ropes" of sticky, stretchy slime out of its face! They tangle around the victim and glue it down so that it can't escape.

Time for dinner! The velvet worm bites a hole in a soft part of the prey and injects some of its saliva to start dissolving the prey's insides. While waiting, the worm enjoys an appetizer: its own slime! The slime contains useful protein, so why waste it? The worm gobbles it up to recycle for next time. Then it moves on to its paralyzed, liquefying main course.

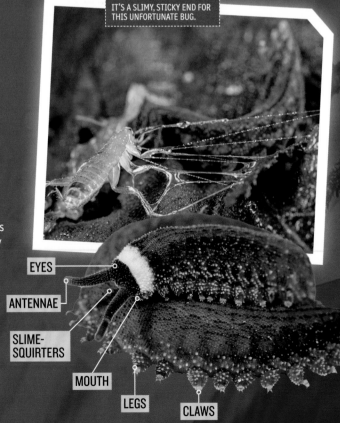

IT'S A SLIMY, STICKY END FOR THIS UNFORTUNATE BUG.

EYES

ANTENNAE

SLIME-SQUIRTERS

MOUTH

LEGS

CLAWS

YOU CAN SEE A LITTLE OF THE SEA STAR'S STOMACH IN THIS PHOTO.

THOUGH SEA STARS DO HAVE EYES, THEY DON'T HAVE A BRAIN!

THE FRESHEST FOOD

SOME HUNTERS LIKE THEIR PREY AS FRESH AS POSSIBLE—SO FRESH, IT'S ACTUALLY *STILL ALIVE*.

✂ A TARANTULA HAWK WASP PARALYZES A TARANTULA WITH HER POWERFUL STING AND THEN DRAGS IT INTO HER BURROW. THERE SHE LAYS AN EGG ON IT, SO THAT WHEN HER BABY HATCHES (SHE HAS JUST ONE AT A TIME), IT CAN FEED ON THE STILL-LIVING SPIDER.

✂ *EPOMIS* GROUND BEETLE LARVAE WAVE THEIR ANTENNAE TO ATTRACT HUNGRY FROGS. WHEN THE FROG TRIES TO GRAB THE LARVA, IT DODGES OUT OF THE WAY, LATCHES ON TO THE FROG'S SKIN, AND STARTS EATING IT ALIVE!

✂ WHEN THE NORTHERN SHORT-TAILED SHREW BITES, IT INJECTS POISON SALIVA THAT PARALYZES PREY. THAT MEANS IT CAN BAG A MEAL LARGER THAN ITSELF OR SAVE FRESH VICTIMS IN ITS BURROW FOR LATER.

DEADLY HUG of Horror

You know you should keep your mouth closed while eating—no one wants to see what's going on in there—so you can be pretty sure they don't want to see the inside of your stomach, either. Apparently, no one told that to sea stars!

Those five (or more) arms aren't just for crawling around. Each arm has a simple eye at the end and can also detect the smell of prey in the water. When an arm senses something tasty, like a clam or mussel, it pulls the rest of the star toward it. All the arms wrap around the mollusk's shell and use suction power to pull it open. Then the sea star pushes its stomach out through its mouth to digest and soak up the meat inside. Once sated, the sea star pulls its stomach back in.

Nasty ASSASSINS

Imagine you're a ladybug or caterpillar, wandering around on a leaf, when suddenly—*yowch!*—something's stuck in your back! It's the long, beak-shaped mouth of an assassin bug. Before you know it, it's injected chemicals to dissolve your insides, so it can slurp them back up in liquid form.

Many assassin bugs simply creep up on their prey, stab them, and enjoy an instant bug smoothie. Others have even sneakier hunting methods ...

❀ The thread-legged bug gently plucks the strings of spiderwebs to mimic a struggling fly. When the spider comes over to catch the supposed fly, the assassin bug attacks!

❀ The feather-legged bug releases a tasty goop to attract ants. The ants come to eat it and—you guessed it—they're lunch.

❀ None of this is quite gross enough for another ant-killing assassin bug. After sucking out the insides of its ant prey, it stacks their dried-out bodies on its back to act as camouflage!

BESIDES THEIR GROSS HUNTING HABITS, TARANTULA HAWK WASPS HAVE THE MOST PAINFUL STING (FOR HUMANS) OF ANY INSECT. SO DON'T GET TOO CLOSE!

HEH HEH HEH, NO ONE WILL GUESS IT'S ME!

DISGUSTING DEFENSES

IT'S AN ANIMAL-EAT-ANIMAL WORLD OUT THERE, AND CRITTERS NEED TO FIND GOOD WAYS TO STAY SAFE OR DISCOURAGE THEIR WOULD-BE PREDATORS. These defenses can include quills, claws, camouflage, and … poop?! Well, as you've discovered in this book, there's a lot of gross stuff in your body. So we guess these animals might as well make the best of it!

HUMANS HAVE ACTUALLY USED POOP AS A WEAPON TOO. THE ANCIENT SCYTHIANS, FROM CENTRAL ASIA, DIPPED THEIR ARROWS IN A MIXTURE OF POOP, BLOOD, AND MUSHED-UP SNAKES TO POISON ENEMIES.

WASTE WEAPONS

Poop is gross … so it stands to reason that it makes a great weapon for grossing out hungry hunters. A baby tortoise beetle, for example, simply poops on itself! It sticks out its long, telescopic poop tube, and it poops onto the tip of its own tail. The larva's tail has a special "fecal fork" to hold a big clump of poop over its back. This puts off most predators—but if they do get too close, the larva can use the poop pile as a weapon and give them a good whack with it.

The chick of the hoopoe, a type of bird, goes one further. It will squirt its gloopy liquid poop at any enemy that disturbs or scares it while it's sitting in its nest.

It works underwater too. When danger threatens, sperm whales can shoot out a brown poopy liquid. They then use their tails to swish it around, making the water cloudy (so it's harder for the predator to see), and probably pretty stinky as well.

THIS TORTOISE BEETLE LARVA HAS ITS SMELLY POOP SHIELD AT THE READY.

KILLER PUKE

Vomit smells bad ... and fish-scented vomit smells *really* bad. That's what you could end up covered with if you disturb a baby fulmar. These seabirds leave their chicks alone in their nests while they go fishing. To deter predators, the chick can squirt a stream of bright orange, oily, gruesome-smelling puke a distance of up to eight feet (2.5 m). The stench of the puke is enough to put anyone off—but for hunting birds, the worst is yet to come. The oily barf clogs up and damages their feathers, so they can't dive for fish, and sometimes this kills them.

WATCH OUT ... OH NO, TOO LATE! YOU JUST GOT SPLATTERED WITH FISHY FULMAR VOMIT.

SCIENTISTS WHO CLIMB CLIFFS TO STUDY AND MONITOR SEABIRDS LIVE IN FEAR OF THE FULMAR CHICK'S SICK TRICK. IF THEY DO GET HIT, THEIR CLOTHES SMELL SO TERRIBLE THEY HAVE TO THROW THEM AWAY.

GORY GROSS-OUT

What could be grosser than a stream of poop or puke? How about blood? The horned lizard has special chambers under its eyes, where blood collects. If it's in danger from a predator, the lizard can build up pressure in the blood bag, and then squeeze and squirt it out at high speed, right at its enemy's face. Horned lizards only do this if they have to, as it can mean losing up to a third of all the blood in their body. If you did that, you'd be squirting out enough blood to fill a medium-size soda bottle!

SPLAT! A HORNED LIZARD HAS A BLOODY DEFENSE.

ANIMALS WITH GUTS

These defenses may be gross, but as far as a sea cucumber is concerned, they're just for beginners! This seabed-dwelling animal, related to sea stars, deals with dangerous predators by shooting a pile of its own intestines and other internal organs right out of its butt. The tangled mass of gut tubes may scare the hunter away. If not, the tubes are also sticky and can entangle and trap the enemy.

After doing this, the sea cucumber doesn't suck its insides back in. They dissolve and break off—and the cucumber just grows itself a new set.

A SEA CUCUMBER HAS A GUTSY DEFENSE.

SPIT TAKE

SOME ANIMALS AREN'T BLESSED WITH SUCH SOPHISTICATED DEFENSE MECHANISMS, SO THEY RESORT TO PLAIN OLD SPITTING INSTEAD.

- CAMELS ARE FAMOUS FOR THEIR GRUMPINESS. IF A CAMEL IS ANNOYED OR FEELS THREATENED, IT WILL COLLECT SALIVA AND GROSS-SMELLING STOMACH JUICES IN ITS MOUTH AND THEN SHOOT THEM OUT.

- LLAMAS ALSO LOVE TO SPIT, BUT MAINLY DO IT AT EACH OTHER—FOR EXAMPLE, TO SCARE ANOTHER LLAMA AWAY FROM SOME FOOD. FEMALES ALSO SPIT AT MALES TO SAY, "NO THANKS, I DON'T WANT TO BE YOUR MATE!"

- THE MOST DANGEROUS SPITTER IS THE SPITTING COBRA, A SNAKE THAT CAN SHOOT VENOM OUT OF ITS FANGS. IT HAS AMAZING AIM AND CAN FIRE THE VENOM STRAIGHT AT ITS ENEMIES' EYES, FROM UP TO SIX FEET (ALMOST 2 M) AWAY.

A SPITTING COBRA SHOOTS VENOM FROM ITS FANGS.

STINKY SWEAT

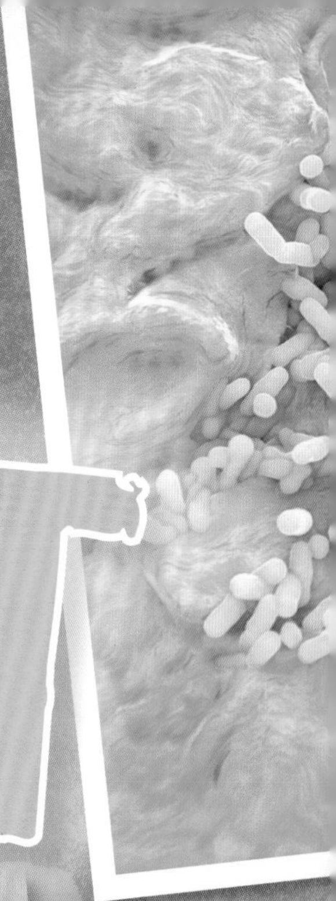

OK, MAYBE YOU DON'T WANT TO HEAR THIS, BUT ... YOU'RE LEAKING! All over your body (well, almost all over) are millions of tiny holes called sweat pores. They lead to sweat glands, which are designed to release liquid sweat onto your skin. When you get too hot and need to cool down, you sweat a lot—but you actually sweat a little bit all the time. You might think you're perfectly dry, but you're wrong!

IF YOU'VE BEEN EATING STRONG, SPICY FOOD LIKE GARLIC OR CHILIES, THEIR SCENTS CAN COME OUT IN YOUR SWEAT TOO!

SLATHERED IN SWEAT

IN SWELTERING HOT WEATHER, OR WHEN YOU'VE BEEN EXERCISING A LOT, YOU'LL SOON FIND YOURSELF COVERED IN SWEAT. Your body needs to stay at a certain temperature—about 99°F (37°C)—so, when it senses you overheating, the sweat glands get to work. In just one hour in the heat, one person's sweat glands can churn out up to eight cups (2 L) of sweat. Top athletes pushing themselves to the limit will sweat even more.

How does being soaked in sweat help? When sweat evaporates into the air, this releases energy in the form of heat from your skin. And you cool down! (This is why being wet always makes you feel colder, by the way.) But even when you're not hot, your body still sweats a little to keep your skin slightly damp, so it doesn't dry out.

USING YOUR MUSCLES MAKES THEM WARM UP, WHICH IS WHY EXERCISE CAUSES SWEATING.

OH NO, B.O.!

SWEATING ITSELF ISN'T REALLY GROSS—IT'S ESSENTIAL AND HEALTHY. When sweat first pops out of your sweat pores, it isn't stinky at all. It's mostly water, with some salt, oils, and other chemicals.

It's only when sweat—or someone's sweaty socks or sports gear—has been hanging around for a while that it really starts to smell bad. This is because after a while, sweat-loving bacteria start feasting on the chemicals in the sweat and making bad-smelling waste. So the smell of sweaty, stale body odor is actually the smell of bacteria poop.

Humans have two main types of sweat glands: eccrine and apocrine. Eccrine glands are more common. They're found all over the body, and they release more watery sweat. Apocrine glands are found in just a few areas—especially the armpits! They release a thicker, milky type of sweat that contains more fats and oils, and this type gets much smellier when the bacteria turn up to chow down. That explains why armpits can be super stinky!

FEEDING FRENZY! THIS PICTURE OF A PORE SHOWS HOW BACTERIA GATHER AND GROW WHERE THERE'S SWEAT TO BE GOBBLED UP.

SWEAT ZONES

AS YOU MAY HAVE NOTICED, SOME PARTS OF THE BODY ARE SWEATIER THAN OTHERS. The areas with the most sweat glands are the palms of your hands, the soles of your feet, and your forehead. An adult man's feet can drip out up to two cups (0.5 L) of sweat per day! This is why unwashed feet can get very smelly. Even though the sweat there is the weaker, watery type, there's plenty of it for the bacteria to feast on.

STANDOUT SWEATERS

DID YOU KNOW THAT HUMANS ARE THE SWEATIEST ANIMALS IN THE WORLD? MANY ANIMALS HARDLY SWEAT AT ALL, BUT HERE ARE A FEW SWEATY ONES ...

- HORSES HAVE MOSTLY APOCRINE GLANDS (THE ONES THAT MAKE THE THICKER, SMELLIER TYPE OF SWEAT). WHEN A HORSE RUNS, ITS THICK, MILKY SWEAT FOAMS UP INTO A WHITE LATHER.

- GORILLAS HAVE SWEATY, SMELLY ARMPITS, JUST LIKE HUMANS DO.

- HIPPOS WERE ONCE THOUGHT TO SWEAT BLOOD. IN FACT, THEIR SKIN RELEASES DROPS OF A REDDISH SUBSTANCE, WHICH ACTS AS A GERM-KILLER AND SUNSCREEN.

SWEAT BEES ARE SMALL BEES THAT LOVE THE SALTY TASTE OF HUMAN SWEAT. SO THEY SIT ON OUR SKIN TO SLURP IT UP!

GET A GRIP!

IF YOU'VE EVER BROKEN OUT INTO A "COLD SWEAT," YOU'LL KNOW THAT YOU DON'T NEED TO BE HOT TO GET SWEATY. It can also happen when you're scared or nervous. Scientists think this has to do with sweat's other useful role: helping us grip things. If something scary happens, you might need to run away. Having damp skin, especially on your hands and feet, could give you a better grip and help you run or climb to make your escape. (This still happens, even though we mostly wear shoes these days! It's been built into our bodies since prehistoric times.)

A MAGGOTY MOUTHFUL

NASTY
GROSS
EWW
DISGUSTING
YUCK-O-METER

MMMMMM, CHEESE! DRIPPING FROM A PIZZA, MELTING ON A BURGER, OR FILLING A DELICIOUS SANDWICH, CHEESE IS A FOOD MOST PEOPLE ENJOY. But you'd have to be a seriously devoted cheese lover to try Sicily's famous *casu marzu*, also known as maggot cheese. Yep, it's runny, stinky cheese that's brimming with real live maggots—that is, the larvae, or babies, of flies.

Making MAGGOT CHEESE

In Sicily, an Italian island, making casu marzu is a tradition that goes back generations. The process begins with sheep's milk, which is made into cheese, then left to ripen. A few weeks later, a hole is cut in the rind, and the cheese is left outdoors to attract the cheese fly—an insect that easily sniffs out tasty dairy products, where it lays its eggs.

(In fact, this could happen to most types of cheese, if you left them out long enough. That's why you're supposed to wrap cheese up and store it in the refrigerator!)

Once the eggs hatch, the tiny maggots emerge and start chowing on the cheese. As it passes through their bodies, chemicals in the maggots' stomachs break the cheese down into a soft, gloopy mess. Once it is pooped out, the cheese becomes ... extra tasty!

THIS FLY'S BABIES LOVE TO LIVE IN CHEESE.

WHEN THE CHEESE IS READY, IT'S SO RUNNY THAT DROPS OF LIQUID SEEP OUT OF THE SIDES. THEY ARE KNOWN AS *LAGRIMA*, MEANING "TEARS" IN ITALIAN.

So Disgusting, IT'S ILLEGAL!

Maggot cheese has actually been banned, and is no longer sold in Sicily's grocery stores. This is because the maggots can sometimes survive being swallowed and set up home in a person's insides. (However, devoted fans say they avoid this problem by simply making sure they chew the maggots really well.)

It's rumored that some people still make and eat the forbidden cheese in private. It's so delicious, they're prepared to risk breaking the law for a mouthful of maggots!

THE MAGGOTS ARE ONLY ABOUT ONE-QUARTER INCH (6.4 MM) LONG, SEE-THROUGH, AND KIND OF CHEESE-COLORED DUE TO ALL THE CHEESE THEY'VE EATEN.

CHEESE, Please!

As you *very sadly* can't try casu marzu for yourself (we know you're devastated), you'll just have to rely on our handy guide to eating and enjoying maggot cheese. If it ever becomes legal again, you'll know what to do!

1. Before starting, do you wear glasses? Good. If not, consider some goggles, or at least shield your eyes with your hand. The maggots in the cheese don't just wriggle and squirm—they can actually jump six inches (15 cm) in the air, and they often aim for your face as you try to take a bite.

2. Spread the cheese on some nice crispy Sicilian flatbread, or *pane carasau*, and dive in! The taste is said to be very spicy and stingy, like extra-strong blue cheese, but even more taste-bud-tingling.

3. Chew it properly to make sure none of those sneaky maggots make it down your throat alive.

4. However, don't eat the cheese if the maggots have died! That means the cheese is too rotten and not OK to eat.

NO, THAT'S NOT POOP— IT'S MILBENKÄSE.

CREEPY-CRAWLY CHEESE

CASU MARZU ISN'T THE ONLY BUG-FILLED CHEESE. IF YOU LIKE THE SOUND OF IT, CONSIDER THESE ALTERNATIVE OPTIONS!

SALTARELLO
SEVERAL OTHER AREAS OF ITALY HAVE THEIR OWN MAGGOTY CHEESE VARIETIES. SALTARELLO COMES FROM THE FRIULI REGION IN NORTHERN ITALY AND SHARES ITS NAME WITH A DANCE THAT INVOLVES LEAPING UP AND DOWN, JUST LIKE THE HOPPING MAGGOTS.

MILBENKÄSE
MEANING "MITE CHEESE," THIS GERMAN CHEESE IS MADE BY PUTTING FRESH SOFT CHEESE IN A BOX WITH SOME FLOUR AND HUNDREDS OF TINY CHEESE MITES. BECAUSE THE MITES ARE RELATED TO SPIDERS, THE CHEESE IS ALSO KNOWN AS *SPINNENKÄSE*, OR "SPIDER CHEESE." AS THE MITES FEAST ON THE CHEESE, IT TURNS FROM YELLOW TO BROWN, THEN BLACK.

MIMOLETTE
THIS IS THE FRENCH VERSION OF MITE CHEESE. IT'S SHAPED INTO A BALL AND IS ORANGE ON THE INSIDE, WITH GRAY, MITE-NIBBLED SKIN.

SERIOUSLY STUFFED ANIMALS

YUCK-O-METER

EWW · GROSS · NASTY · DISGUSTING

HAVE YOU EVER SEEN A STUFFED BIRD IN A MUSEUM, STARING AT YOU WITH ITS GLASSY EYES? Or animals positioned in a lifelike display, like a cougar leaping to catch a rabbit? These are real deceased creatures, but they don't decay, start to smell, or get eaten by ants or bacteria. That's thanks to the amazing—but admittedly, kind of gross—art of taxidermy.

A STUFFY HISTORY

Taxidermy first became popular in the 1700s, when explorers began bringing newly discovered animal specimens back from their travels. Before photography existed, this was the best way to keep a record of each discovery for scientific purposes.

Eventually, in Victorian times, it became trendy to have your own stuffed animal collection at home. Before people began to understand the need for conservation, they often believed that having preserved rare animals was a sign of wealth or prestige. Some people also kept collections of birds or insects, and others paid to have their pets preserved after they died, so that they could still have them around.

A TAXIDERMIST AT WORK

WE OFTEN CALL TAXIDERMY "STUFFED" ANIMALS, BUT TAXIDERMISTS THEMSELVES PREFER TO USE THE WORD "MOUNTED." A FINISHED PIECE IS CALLED A "MOUNT."

MUSEUMS OFTEN USE TAXIDERMY TO PROMOTE CONSERVATION.

LIFELIKE EXHIBITS

In the early 1900s, many people had never seen a tiger or an elephant. Television hadn't yet been invented, and not everyone could afford to take a vacation to faraway destinations. Instead, museums featured displays full of stuffed animals. These creature features were the most realistic experience many people could have, and helped educate the public about animals across the world.

Today, museums often still use taxidermy. They often update the practice by combining stuffed animals with digital displays, or pose the stuffed animals somewhere unexpected, like in mid-air above the visitors! These taxidermy displays allow visitors to experience rare animals up close, and help encourage conservation and the protection of endangered species. On top of that, some museums hold taxidermy workshops, where you can get involved and even try it out yourself!

BACK FROM THE DEAD

A taxidermist turns dead animals into realistic, lifelike models, preserving them so they don't rot. To do this job, people need a strong stomach, and zero fear of dealing with dead things or touching animals' insides. And it also takes a lot of detailed handiwork and artistic skill. Do you think you might want to be a taxidermist? Here's what you'd have to do:

1. First, you need a dead animal—usually a creature that's been hunted, run over, or has died naturally. Taxidermists often stick their animals in the freezer to keep them fresh until they're ready to start work.

2. The taxidermist carefully cuts the animal open and peels off its skin all in one piece (gulp!), along with its fur or feathers. The rest of the body is thrown away, except for (occasionally) the skull and some other bones.

3. The taxidermist uses a chemical such as borax to preserve the skin and stop it from rotting and starting to smell.

4. Next, the taxidermist makes a form—an animal-shaped model to fit the skin onto. Forms can be made from wool, cotton wool, wire, wood, clay, plastic, or a mixture of materials.

5. Nearly done—except that the skin didn't come with the eyeballs attached. So the taxidermist adds glass eyes to the form, then covers it with the skin so that the eyes show through. They sew the skin back together with tiny, neat stitches.

SICKENING SURGERY

YUCK-O-METER

EWW · GROSS · NASTY · DISGUSTING

HAS ALL THIS GREAT GROSSNESS GIVEN YOU A HORRIBLE, POUNDING HEADACHE THAT YOU JUST CAN'T GET RID OF? Well, be grateful you're alive nowadays, so you don't have to have a piece of your skull chopped out in order to make a hole directly through to your brain! This treatment, called trepanning, was just one of the strange and sickening surgical procedures that people used to rely on. Dive in for more!

Time for TREPANNING

More than 8,000 years ago, trepanning took off as a medical treatment. Scientists have discovered hundreds of skulls across the world with holes neatly cut or bored into them. To us, this seems like a terrible idea—why would people purposely put a hole in their head?

Experts think trepanning was most likely used to treat terrible headaches like migraines, or epilepsy, a disease that causes fits or seizures. Ancient humans probably reasoned that these must be caused by something in the brain that needed to get out—an evil spirit, perhaps.

Did trepanning work? Experts don't know for certain, but some skulls show evidence that the bone around the hole had regrown and healed. That means that some patients did survive the experience at least!

You may be surprised to hear that trepanning actually continued into modern times. In the 1600s, and even up until the 1800s, doctors used special contraptions called trephines for drilling into patients' heads. And it's occasionally still performed today, to relieve a buildup of blood or pressure in the brain. Maybe those ancient doctors were right after all!

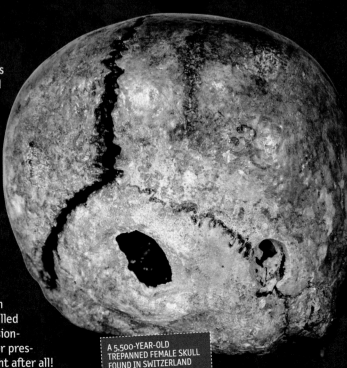

A 5,500-YEAR-OLD TREPANNED FEMALE SKULL FOUND IN SWITZERLAND

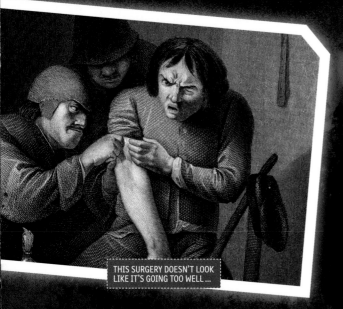

THIS SURGERY DOESN'T LOOK LIKE IT'S GOING TOO WELL ...

SURGERY and a SHAVE

These days, surgery is performed by specially trained doctors in hospitals. In medieval Europe, things weren't so formal. Doctors didn't perform surgery—barbers did! After all, cutting hair and shaving beards meant they always had plenty of sharp knives and razorblades around. Each barber-surgeon trained as an apprentice and learned to do a range of surgical tasks, including ...

* Sewing up cuts and wounds
* Pulling out rotten teeth
* Lancing (cutting open) big pus-filled boils
* Bloodletting—that is, cutting open a vein to let some blood out (see page 20)
* Trepanning holes in people's heads
* Amputating fingers or even whole limbs.

Barber-surgeons went with armies into battle, and they visited castles and monasteries to offer their services. But they also had shops that anyone could drop by. Before the 1300s, barber-surgeons in London advertised their services with gruesome displays of bowls of blood or pulled-out teeth in their shop windows. When this was (thankfully) banned, another sign developed: a red-and-white-striped pole, which represented flowing blood and white bandages. Many barbers still have these poles today (though they no longer slice their customers open)!

Who Let the DIRT IN?

For most of the history of surgery, no one knew that tiny, invisible germs could get into the body and lead to infections and even death. Surgery was carried out in filthy rooms, where discarded body parts were lying around, and performed with gross, dirty tools that had just been used on other people.

It wasn't until the late 1800s that scientists figured out how germs make us sick. British surgeon Joseph Lister was the first to spray wounds and tools with disinfectant, wear gloves to perform surgery, and make sure everyone washed their hands. At first, other doctors sneered at him, but his methods led the way to the modern, squeaky-clean operating rooms we have today.

AN OPERATING ROOM IS SOMETIMES CALLED AN OPERATING THEATER BECAUSE THE ROOMS WHERE SURGERIES TOOK PLACE USED TO ACTUALLY BE THEATERS SO STUDENTS COULD WATCH AND LEARN!

OFF With His Leg!

Before modern medicine, wounds often became infected with germs. Sometimes a foot, hand, or leg would get gangrene—meaning it actually started to die—and turn a ghoulish blackish green color. The only option was to cut off the bad body part in what is called an amputation. The same happened if an arm or leg was badly crushed or damaged in a battle.

Whether an amputation took place on a battlefield, on a ship at sea, or in the barber-surgeon's shop, it was a horrendous ordeal. Sometimes herbs and chemicals were used as painkillers, but they didn't work very well. So a team of helpers had to hold the patient down, while the surgeon sawed the limb off and sewed up the skin.

THIS WON'T HURT (MUCH)

TODAY WE HAVE ANESTHETICS, WHICH PREVENT PAIN AND ALLOW THE PATIENT TO BE UNCONSCIOUS DURING SURGERY. BEFORE THEY WERE INVENTED, THERE WAS A RANGE OF OTHER TERRIBLE-SOUNDING OPTIONS. A PATIENT COULD BE ...

* PUNCHED REALLY HARD TO BE KNOCKED OUT.
* GIVEN A STICK OR A PIECE OF LEATHER TO BITE DOWN ON. THIS DIDN'T STOP THE PAIN BUT WAS SUPPOSED TO HELP PATIENTS PUT UP WITH IT.
* STUNG WITH NETTLES. POSSIBLY THE WORST IDEA OF ALL, THIS WAS SUPPOSED TO DISTRACT THE PATIENT FROM THE PAIN OF SURGERY!
* HYPNOTIZED. THIS SOMETIMES WORKED WELL, BUT OFTEN IT DIDN'T.

GROSS PLANT GALLERY

YUCK-O-METER

EWW · GROSS · NASTY · DISGUSTING

AHH, THE JOYS OF NATURE. Wait, what's that over there—stinky vegetables? A plant with eyeballs? Goop-squirting cucumbers?! Read on to enjoy a ghoulish garden of horticultural horrors.

DOLL'S EYE PLANT

LATIN NAME: *Actaea pachypoda*
SIZE: Up to 2 feet (0.6 m) high

Ever get that feeling that someone—or something—is watching you? This plant, also known as the white baneberry, does have flowers, but in summer they are replaced by its spooky, eyelike white berries.

WARNING!
The berries aren't just weird-looking, they're also deadly poisonous. Do not touch!

BLACK BAT FLOWER

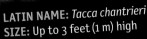

LATIN NAME: *Tacca chantrieri*
SIZE: Up to 3 feet (1 m) high

Look after your black bat plant carefully, and it will reward you by sprouting a terrifying flower. Resembling a huge black bat, the flower is typically 12 inches (30 cm) across, with up to 30 long dangly tentacles, or "whiskers," hanging out of it.

WARNING!
According to local superstitions in Southeast Asia, where this plant comes from, looking at the flower for too long could bring you bad luck.

LATIN NAME: *Proboscidea louisianica*
SIZE: Up to 3 feet (1 m) high

When this plant grows seeds, they form inside long, hooked, black seed pods that look as if they're trying to grab you as you walk past. And actually, they are! These plants spread their seeds by hooking on to animals' feet (or humans' pants), so they are then carried far and wide.

WARNING!
The plant also covers itself with sticky slime to guard against insect pests. Touch it and you'll be a sticky mess.

DEVIL'S CLAW
PLANT

LATIN NAME: *Ecballium elaterium*
SIZE: Up to 2 feet (0.6 m) across

This plant may look fairly innocent, but those green oval fruits build up huge amounts of pressure inside. At any moment, they can explode, popping off their stalks and shooting a stream of seeds and gelatinous liquid up to 20 feet (6 m). Look out!

WARNING!
Do not add this plant to your salad; it's nothing like an edible cucumber. It's prickly, gloopy, and poisonous, and it can give people dangerously deadly diarrhea.

SQUIRTING
CUCUMBER

LATIN NAME:
Raoulia eximia
SIZE: Up to 6 feet (1.8 m) wide and 3 feet (0.9 m) high

VEGETABLE
SHEEP

High in the cold, windy mountains of New Zealand, you might spot, in the distance, a flock of sheep clinging to the rocky slopes. But wait a minute, those aren't sheep! They're vegetable sheep: a flowering plant that forms thick, woolly-looking clumps.

WARNING!
Sheepdogs sometimes get very confused and try to chase and round up the vegetable sheep. That's how sheeplike the plants are, despite having no heads, tails, or feet.

STINKING TOE
TREE

LATIN NAME: *Hymenaea courbaril*
SIZE: Up to 130 feet (40 m) tall

This tropical tree grows toes! OK, its seedpods grow in clusters that just *look* like big, stubby toes. They also smell really bad, but once you crack them open, the powdery pulp inside is said to taste delicious.

WARNING!
The pods are rock-hard and heavy, and they can fall off the tree and whack unwary passersby on the head.

LATIN NAME:
Mammillaria elongata cristata
SIZE: Up to 6 inches (15 cm) across

BRAIN
CACTUS

Complete your Halloween-themed plant collection with a cactus that looks exactly like a brain. This cactus is a houseplant that is encouraged to grow in a swirling, brainlike pattern and is perfect for any vegetarian zombies lurking around.

WARNING!
Don't let your brain cactus get too wet or too cold, or it won't survive.

FRIGHTENINGLY FOUL FLIES

YUCK-O-METER

EWW · GROSS · NASTY · DISGUSTING

WHAT'S A TOTALLY GROSS, DISGUSTING, AND EVEN DANGEROUS ANIMAL? Maybe you thought of a venomous snake, a drooling Komodo dragon, or a killer jelly-fish. But get ready to meet a terrifying, nasty creature much smaller than that. In fact, it's probably wandering around your kitchen right now, looking for something to eat. Yep, we're talking about … the common housefly.

Foul Feeding HABITS

So maybe you've noticed some frustrating flies buzzing around your left-out food and casually waved them away. Who cares, right? It's just a tiny, annoying fly. Well, get ready to hurl when you hear what's really happening when that fly lands on your lunch!

1. A hungry housefly sniffs out some food, such as a doughnut, using its smell-sensitive antennae.

2. The fly zeroes in and lands on its feet. Feet that have previously been trailing through some of its other favorite foods, like rotting garbage and dog poop.

3. But wait—this doughnut isn't liquid, so the fly can't eat it. No problem! The fly heaves up some saliva and vomit onto the food, which starts to dissolve it. To help things along, the fly stamps on the messy mush with its germ-laden feet.

4. Finally, the fly has created a nice vomit, saliva, and doughnut soup. Now it can plunge its spongy mouth into the liquidized food to slurp it up. Delicious!

5. Oh, but we're not done yet. Because flies only eat liquids, they poop every few minutes. So the fly will probably take a quick poop on the doughnut as well, before flying away.

STILL WANT THAT DOUGHNUT?

MARVELOUS MAGGOTS

MAGGOTS ARE THE LARVAE, OR BABIES, OF FLIES. MOST PEOPLE FIND THEM SUPER DISGUSTING. THAT COULD BE BECAUSE THEY'RE SEEN AS A SIGN OF DECAY AND GERMS, THANKS TO THE GROSS PLACES WE FIND THEM. HOWEVER, MAGGOTS CAN BE REALLY USEFUL TOO …

- PEOPLE WHO GO FISHING LOVE MAGGOTS, AS THEY MAKE GREAT BAIT. SOME FISHING FANS LIKE TO WARM UP THEIR MAGGOTS IN THEIR MOUTHS BEFORE USING THEM!

- MAGGOTS CAN ALSO BE USED TO MUNCH UP FOOD WASTE. ONCE THEY ARE NICE AND FAT, THE MAGGOTS ARE THEN TURNED INTO FOOD FOR FARM ANIMALS, WHILE THEIR POOP CAN BE MADE INTO FERTILIZER. GENIUS!

- MAGGOTS LOVE TO MUNCH DEAD, ROTTING FLESH. AND IT TURNS OUT THIS CAN BE VERY HANDY IN HOSPITALS! PEOPLE SUFFERING FROM SERIOUS BURNS OR GANGRENE (WHEN PART OF THE BODY STARTS TO ROT) SOMETIMES HAVE MAGGOTS PUT ONTO THEIR WOUNDS TO NIBBLE AWAY THE DEAD FLESH. THESE MEDICAL MAGGOTS ARE SPECIALLY BRED IN CLEAN CONDITIONS, SO THEY DON'T CARRY GERMS.

Horrible HANGOUTS

Why do flies buzz around poop and dead animals? For flies, this stuff contains useful food. In fact, flies are excellent at extracting food wherever they can find it, whether that's from your doughnut, your dog's feeding bowl, or your dog's poop. They also lay their eggs in places like this, so that their babies, or maggots, can feed on it when they hatch.

Different flies have different favorite spots. Houseflies like trash, while bluebottles (similar to houseflies, but with a shiny blue body) lay their eggs in dead animal bodies. Tiny fruit flies prefer rotting fruit and vegetables, so they're common around compost heaps.

DISGUSTING Diseases

With all these heinous habits, it's no surprise that flies spread diseases. A fly landing on food could be carrying dozens of different types of germs. Eating food or drinking water contaminated by flies can make people seriously sick with illnesses like cholera, typhoid, or salmonella poisoning. The fly family also includes biting and bloodsucking flies such as mosquitoes and tsetse flies. These spread killer diseases like malaria, yellow fever, and sleeping sickness. This makes the fly family the world's biggest killers.

THE STRANGE AND SMELLY MIDDLE AGES

HAVE YOU EVER WANTED TO BE A PRINCE OR PRINCESS, SWANNING AROUND IN A MEDIEVAL STONE CASTLE? Well, you might want to reconsider. Today, the Middle Ages of Western Europe, spanning from around A.D. 500 to 1500, are thought of as dirty, smelly, and deadly. Actually, it wasn't always that bad—but compared to today, it certainly was pretty gross. And it was even worse if you weren't royalty!

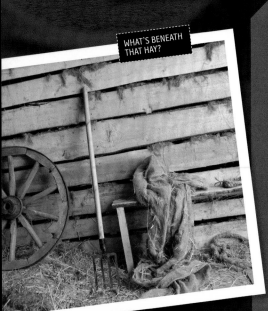

WHAT'S BENEATH THAT HAY?

EAU DE MIDDLE AGES

If you jumped into a time machine right now and stepped out into Europe's Middle Ages, the first thing you'd notice would be the smell. People washed themselves and their clothes far less often than we do today. Rich people might take a bath once a month, or sometimes more often—but some of the poorest people never bathed! They just washed their hands and faces with a cloth.

Doing the laundry was a big job, as there were no washing machines, and some people went for months without washing their clothes. In fact, a lot of people had only one outfit, which meant it would just keep getting dirtier until it was finally washed!

Their homes were often stinky too. A typical peasant's house didn't have a floor, just bare earth. To make it softer and warmer, people put down hay or grasslike plants called rushes. When the flooring became worn out, they just added more on top. After a few months, tons of gross stuff had started to gather at ground level. Besides the old rotting plants, there were mouse and rat droppings, spilled drinks and food, pee and poop from pets and farm animals that wandered in and out, and even spit and vomit. Unsurprisingly, the floor was home to a whole host of gruesome germs. The filthy floors could actually spread horrible diseases as people and animals tramped to and fro. Now there's a reason to clean your room!

MEDIEVAL MUNCHIES

People in the Middle Ages loved their food, and the wealthy often threw amazing feasts. But the food they liked might seem pretty gross to you today. You might have chicken, rice, and vegetables for dinner, with sweet ice cream for dessert. But in medieval times, sweet and savory foods were often mixed together in one dish.

For example, tasty "Tart de Brymlent" was a pie containing figs, raisins, apples, pears, and prunes, mixed with sugar, and combined with ... salmon. Blancmange, today the name of a dessert, was then a kind of white jelly made of chicken and rice and mixed with sugar, almonds, and rosewater.

The richer you were, the unhealthier your diet often was. Meat, fish, sugar, and white and wheat bread were more expensive, so wealthy people ate them in huge quantities. Poorer people had to make do with whole-meal rye bread, beans, and vegetables such as cabbage and turnips. As we know now, these foods are much better for you, but in the Middle Ages people looked down on them and saw them as unhealthy. They actually avoided salad; they thought it made you sick!

MEDIEVAL FEAST

MEDIEVAL ARMIES SOMETIMES USED CATAPULTS TO FLING THE DISEASED DEAD BODIES OF ANIMALS OVER CASTLE WALLS TO SPREAD DISEASE INSIDE.

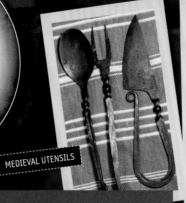
MEDIEVAL UTENSILS

VEGETABLE VENGEANCE

What did people do with vegetables if they didn't eat them? Well, they were often thrown at criminals who were stuck in the stocks. The stocks were a punishment device that held people in place by their legs, usually in a public area. A similar invention, the pillory, held the neck and arms. For small crimes, people were put into the stocks or pillory for a few hours, and passersby could throw things at them. If you got splattered by rotten cabbage, onions, or eggs, you were actually lucky—some people threw stones!

MIND YOUR MANNERS!

CONTRARY TO SOME DEPICTIONS IN MOVIES OR STORIES, MEDIEVAL PEOPLE WEREN'T COMPLETELY WILD, AND THEY HIGHLY VALUED MANNERS—ESPECIALLY DURING FANCY FEASTS. HOWEVER, THEIR IDEAS OF TABLE MANNERS DON'T QUITE MATCH OUR MODERN IDEAS OF POLITE BEHAVIOR! IF YOU ATTENDED A FEAST, YOU'D HAVE TO REMEMBER THESE RULES:

🍴 NEVER SCRATCH YOUR HEAD AT THE TABLE. GROSS! (THIS MIGHT BE BECAUSE LICE COULD FALL OUT OF YOUR HAIR INTO THE FOOD.)

🍴 WHEN YOU'VE CHEWED THE MEAT OFF A BONE, DON'T BE RUDE BY PUTTING THE BONE BACK ON THE PLATE— THROW IT ON THE FLOOR INSTEAD.

🍴 ALWAYS PICK UP FOOD WITH YOUR KNIFE, AND THEN PUT IT IN YOUR MOUTH WITH YOUR FINGERS.

🍴 ONLY BARBARIANS WOULD USE A FORK FOR EATING. FORKS ARE FOR COOKING ONLY; THEY DON'T GO IN YOUR MOUTH!

113

HORRIBLE HUMAN HABITS

WE HUMANS LIKE TO THINK WE'RE A CIVILIZED BUNCH. We live in houses, wear clothes, eat with knives and forks, and behave politely. We're not gross! Or are we?

Ask most people if they love to pick their nails or teeth, peel dead skin off their feet, or eat their own boogers, and they'll probably exclaim, *"Ewwww,* of course not!" But in private, almost everyone does gross stuff some-times! We know they do, because scientists have actually done studies and tests on it. It turns out many people just can't help themselves from prodding, squeezing, and picking at their scabs and pimples.

PICKY PEOPLE

The weird thing is, picking at skin, nails, pimples, and scabs is not good for you. It's pretty weird that many people have an urge to do something that could cause them injury or pain. But scientists say the reasons could go back to prehistoric times, when we lived in a more natural, out-doorsy, and—er—*dirty* state.

In those days, if you saw something on your skin or felt an itch, picking at it made sense. It was much more likely to be something you needed to get rid of, like a creepy-crawly tick, or a biting fly or spider. Maybe some of us still have that ancient urge to pick off anything we can from our bodies.

AARRGGH, GET THAT THING OFF ME!

INSTEAD OF PICKING, WASHING YOUR FACE WELL AND USING ACNE CREAM WILL HELP TO ZAP ZITS.

ANYONE CAN GET ZITS, BUT THEY'RE MOST COMMON FOR TEENAGERS. THAT'S BECAUSE CHANGING HORMONES IN THE BODY CAN MAKE THE SKIN RELEASE EXTRA SEBUM.

SQUEEZE IT, POP IT!

Picking is just one horrible habit, of course. There's also squeezing. Many people just love to squeeze zits until the gunk inside pops or squirts out.

But why do zits pop? Zits form in hair follicles, which are openings in the skin that hairs grow from. You actually have these all over, including on your face, though you can't always see them. Inside each follicle, there's a gland that releases sebum, a kind of yellowish, oily goop that keeps hair and skin soft. If the follicle gets blocked with dead skin cells, sebum can get trapped. If bacteria get in there too, you end up with a sore, inflamed lump full of sebum and germs.

By pushing either side of the zit, one can break the surface and let the gunk burst out. But it can go wrong. Sometimes, the bacteria get pushed farther into the skin instead, making the zit bigger and more painful. And touching zits with fingers can add more bacteria, spread germs around, and create even more spots!

Luckily, if left alone, the zit will eventually pop itself, or just fade away as your body manages to kill the germs. Phew!

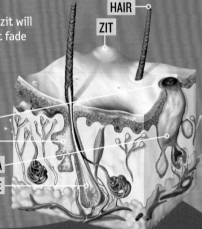

HAIR

ZIT

DEAD SKIN CELLS

SEBUM GLAND

SEBUM AND BACTERIA

HAIR FOLLICLE

TOP HORRENDOUS HABITS

GET READY TO GO *"EEEEEEEWWW!"* HERE ARE SOME OF THE MOST COMMON DISGUSTING PERSONAL HABITS THAT PEOPLE ADMITTED TO IN SURVEYS:

- PICKING YOUR NOSE
- PICKING OFF DEAD SKIN
- PEEING IN THE SHOWER
- PASSING WIND AND PRETENDING IT WASN'T YOU
- SQUEEZING ZITS
- SNIFFING YOUR OWN ARMPITS
- EATING FOOD YOU'VE DROPPED ON THE FLOOR
- WIPING BOOGERS ON WALLS
- EATING BOOGERS

CRACK! CRACK! CRUNCH!

To some people, it's harmless. To others, it's excruciatingly unbearable! It's knuckle-cracking—pulling or bending your fingers (or other body parts) to make them go CRACK!

The sound can be so loud that many people think it's caused by bones cracking. But actually, the "crack" happens inside a joint. Each joint has a sealed bag of oily fluid around it. When you pull or stretch the joint, the pressure inside gets lower, and gas dissolved in the liquid forms a bubble. The bubble suddenly POPS, with a sound that makes some people want to throw up or tear their hair out!

If you're a knuckle-cracker yourself, though, you probably like it. The pop releases tension in the joints, especially for people who use their hands a lot, like crafters or coders. People can get addicted to the relaxing feeling, so they do it over and over.

IT'S OFTEN SAID THAT CRACKING YOUR KNUCKLES WILL GIVE YOU ARTHRITIS. BUT, SO FAR, SCIENTISTS HAVE NOT ACTUALLY FOUND ANY EVIDENCE THAT THIS IS TRUE.

INVISIBLE ENEMIES

YUCK-O-METER — EWW · GROSS · NASTY · DISGUSTING

HOW MANY TIMES HAVE YOU BEEN TOLD TO WASH YOUR HANDS? A LOT, RIGHT? Handwashing, cleaning toilets, cooking meat properly, disinfecting hospital wards—it's all part of our big battle against an army of tiny, invisible, living things—germs. When germs are alive, they can cause diseases, food poisoning, or horrible infections, from everyday colds and flu to nightmare illnesses like rabies and Ebola. But what are they really like? Time to get up close and personal with some of the billions of bacteria and other germs all around us.

E. COLI

(short for *Escherichia coli*)
A common, sausage-shaped bacteria found in human and animal intestines and poop. There are several varieties. Some are harmless, but others can make you really sick and are sometimes fatal. People can catch *E. coli* from unclean food or water, toilets, soil, or handling animals. *This* is why you wash your hands after using the bathroom!

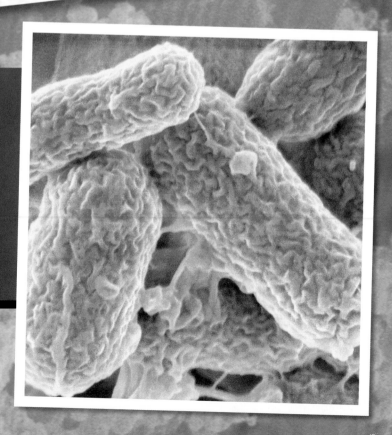

SALMONELLA

One of the most common food-poisoning bacteria, often caught by eating undercooked chicken or pork, it can give you awful stomach cramps and diarrhea. Salmonella use their tentacle-shaped "arms," called flagella, to swim and wriggle around!

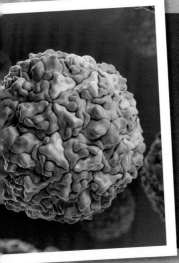

RHINOVIRUS (COMMON COLD)

Colds are caused by viruses, which are tiny microorganisms, smaller even than bacteria. The rhinovirus (meaning "nose virus") gives you a cold when you breathe it in. It attacks cells in your nose and throat, making them sore and swollen. There's no cure, but after a few days of sniffing, sneezing, and dribbling snot everywhere, your body usually manages to overcome and destroy the virus.

BACTERIOPHAGE

The object in this picture might look like some kind of freaky alien robot, but it's actually a natural living thing found here on Earth. It's a type of virus called a bacteriophage, which doesn't attack human cells—it attacks *E. coli* bacteria. (In fact, bacteriophage viruses are usually harmless to us humans.)

THIS IS A MICROSCOPE PHOTO OF THE TIP OF A SYRINGE NEEDLE COVERED IN BACTERIA.

HOW SMALL?

Germs are *very* small. A single bacterium has one cell, and it is much smaller than most human body cells. An *E. coli* bacterium, for example, is about two microns long. A micron is 1/1000 of a millimeter. So you could fit a row of about 3,000 *E. coli*, laid end to end, across your little fingernail. (As long as you washed your hands later, that is!)

Viruses are even smaller, and they are not even made of cells. They force cells to make copies of the virus and then burst open and release them.

LOVE IT ... HATE IT!

WHAT HELPS GERMS GROW AND THRIVE, AND WHAT MAKES THEM STRUGGLE TO SURVIVE? KNOWING THIS CAN HELP YOU KEEP THOSE BUGS AT BAY ...

WHAT GERMS LOVE ...

- **MOISTURE:** GERMS GROW BEST IN DAMP PLACES.
- **FOOD:** BACTERIA LOVE HIGH-PROTEIN FOOD, LIKE MEAT, MILK, AND BEANS.
- **MEDIUM TEMPERATURE:** EXTREME HEAT AND COLD KILL MANY GERMS OR STOP THEM FROM BREEDING.

WHAT GERMS HATE ...

- **CHEMICALS KNOWN AS ACIDS AND ALKALIS** (SUCH AS LEMON JUICE, AN ACID, OR AMMONIA, AN ALKALI): MOST GERM-KILLING CLEANING CHEMICALS ARE STRONG ACIDS OR ALKALIS. GERMS PREFER A NEUTRAL ENVIRONMENT, SOMEWHERE IN THE MIDDLE.
- **YOUR IMMUNE SYSTEM:** STAY HEALTHY, AND YOUR GERM-ZAPPING WHITE BLOOD CELLS WILL BE BETTER AT THEIR JOB.
- **ANTIBIOTICS:** THESE MEDICINES KILL BACTERIA IN THE BODY (ALTHOUGH SOME BACTERIA ARE NOW BECOMING RESISTANT TO THEM).

QUIZ
GERM DETECTIVE

A. GROCERY CART
B. VEGETABLE AISLE
C. CHECKOUT

GRAB YOUR MICROSCOPE AND SWAB KIT—YOU'RE GOING GERM-HUNTING. Germs, as you probably know by now, are all over the place. They have the power to spread diseases, cause infections, and contaminate clean food and water. But those sneaky single-celled critters are also extremely tiny and are usually totally invisible to us humans, so it can be very hard to tell where they're hanging out.

Check out these eight everyday locations, and see if you can guess which is the scuzziest germ hot spot in each place. You might be surprised!

BATHROOM

A. BATH MAT
B. TOILET SEAT
C. TOOTHBRUSH HOLDER

KITCHEN

A. KITCHEN SPONGE
B. TOASTER
C. FLOOR

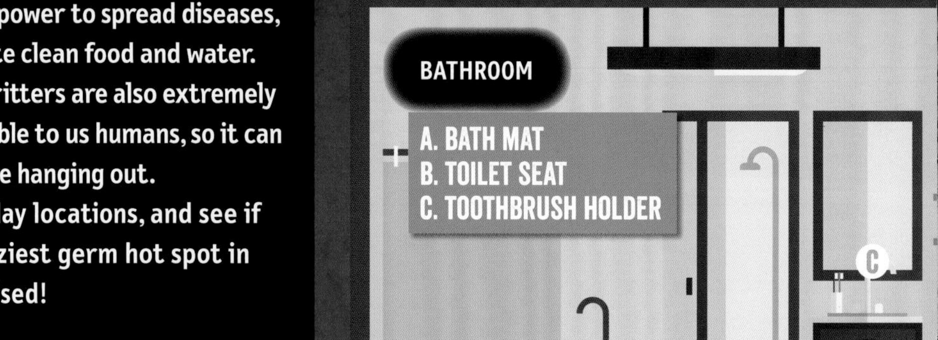

HUMAN SKIN

A. TOENAILS
B. FACE
C. SCALP

Human skin: B. Face. Your face includes your mouth, which is laden with bugs, as well as your eyes, nose, and ears, which all have plenty of their own, and lots of other skin bacteria.

Grocery store: A. Grocery cart. Scientists found a wide range of germs on these, including poop germs, outdoor germs carried in on children's shoes, and mold growing in old food remnants.

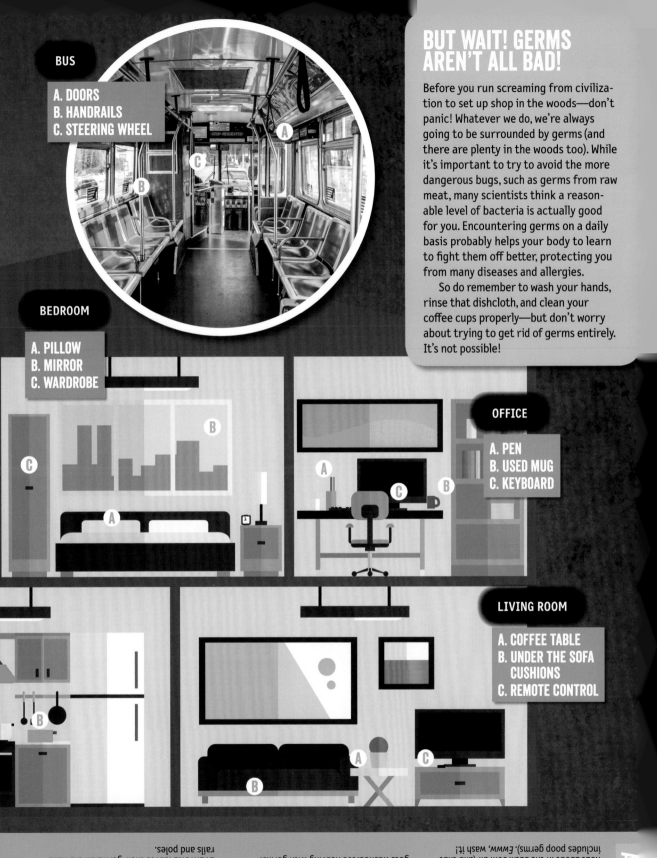

BUS
A. DOORS
B. HANDRAILS
C. STEERING WHEEL

BEDROOM
A. PILLOW
B. MIRROR
C. WARDROBE

OFFICE
A. PEN
B. USED MUG
C. KEYBOARD

LIVING ROOM
A. COFFEE TABLE
B. UNDER THE SOFA CUSHIONS
C. REMOTE CONTROL

BUT WAIT! GERMS AREN'T ALL BAD!

Before you run screaming from civilization to set up shop in the woods—don't panic! Whatever we do, we're always going to be surrounded by germs (and there are plenty in the woods too). While it's important to try to avoid the more dangerous bugs, such as germs from raw meat, many scientists think a reasonable level of bacteria is actually good for you. Encountering germs on a daily basis probably helps your body to learn to fight them off better, protecting you from many diseases and allergies.

So do remember to wash your hands, rinse that dishcloth, and clean your coffee cups properly—but don't worry about trying to get rid of germs entirely. It's not possible!

ANSWERS:

Kitchen: A. Kitchen sponge or dishcloth. It touches all kinds of dirty surfaces and stays damp, allowing germs to breed. To keep it clean, wash and replace it regularly.

Bathroom: C. Toothbrush holder! You might think it's the toilet seat, but people tend to clean the toilet more often. The toothbrush holder collects drips of water and germs from your mouth, plus all the germs that float about in the bathroom air (and that includes poop germs). Ewww, wash it!

Bedroom: A. Pillow. Yup, it's the cozy, comfy place where you rest your head for around one-third of each day! Sweat, sebum, dead skin cells, dust, and dust mites collect in pillows, which is why they need washing and changing often.

Living room: C. Remote control. Everyone touches it, coughs and sneezes on it, and leaves it lying around—but it hardly ever gets washed. It's heaving with germs!

Office: B. Used mug. Office cups get washed with the germy kitchen sponge, and office coffee machines often carry germs too. If an old, dirty mug is left on a desk, it can soon grow all kinds of bacteria and mold. (Keyboards are pretty gross too, though!)

Bus: B. Handrails. Fewer people touch the doors as they're automatic, and only the drivers touch the steering wheel—but EVERYONE leaves their germs on the handrails and poles.

MEET YOUR GROSS HOUSEGUESTS!

YUCK-O-METER
EWW · GROSS · NASTY · DISGUSTING

WHO LIVES IN YOUR HOUSE? YOU, YOUR FAMILY, AND MAYBE A PET OR TWO? Sure—but that's actually just the tip of the iceberg! Your cozy home is also full of a whole bunch of much smaller room-mates. They often like to creep around out of sight, so let's take a closer look at what could be living in your cupboards, carpets, bathroom, or basement …

CLOTHES MOTH

LATIN NAME: *Tineola bisselliella*
SIZE: 1/4 inch (6 mm) long
HANGS OUT: In clothes, blankets, carpets, and soft furnishings
FAVORITE FOODS: The larva (or caterpillar) of the clothes moth eats wool and other natural fibers.
CREATURE FEATURES: The larva spins itself a tube-like nest. Adults look fluffy and dusty.

AAARRGH, GET RID OF IT!
WASH CLOTHES AND FABRICS REG-ULARLY AND HANG THEM OUT IN THE SUN TO BANISH THE MOTHS.

STUDIES HAVE FOUND THAT ROOMS WITH CARPETS HAVE MORE BUGS THAN ROOMS WITHOUT.

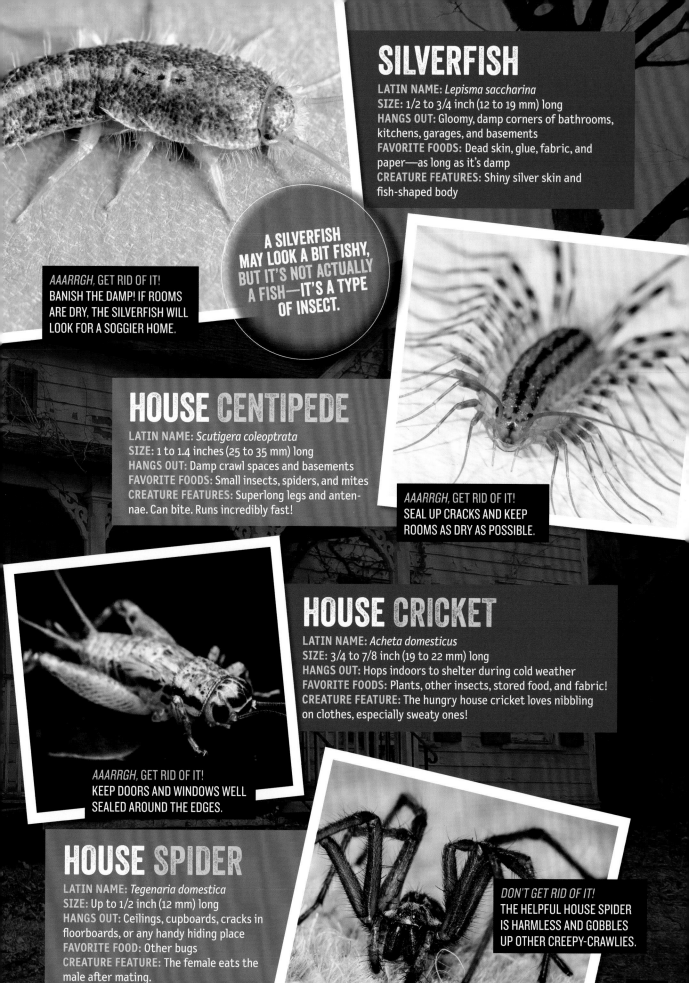

SILVERFISH

LATIN NAME: *Lepisma saccharina*
SIZE: 1/2 to 3/4 inch (12 to 19 mm) long
HANGS OUT: Gloomy, damp corners of bathrooms, kitchens, garages, and basements
FAVORITE FOODS: Dead skin, glue, fabric, and paper—as long as it's damp
CREATURE FEATURES: Shiny silver skin and fish-shaped body

A SILVERFISH MAY LOOK A BIT FISHY, BUT IT'S NOT ACTUALLY A FISH—IT'S A TYPE OF INSECT.

AAARRGH, GET RID OF IT!
BANISH THE DAMP! IF ROOMS ARE DRY, THE SILVERFISH WILL LOOK FOR A SOGGIER HOME.

HOUSE CENTIPEDE

LATIN NAME: *Scutigera coleoptrata*
SIZE: 1 to 1.4 inches (25 to 35 mm) long
HANGS OUT: Damp crawl spaces and basements
FAVORITE FOODS: Small insects, spiders, and mites
CREATURE FEATURES: Superlong legs and antennae. Can bite. Runs incredibly fast!

AAARRGH, GET RID OF IT!
SEAL UP CRACKS AND KEEP ROOMS AS DRY AS POSSIBLE.

HOUSE CRICKET

LATIN NAME: *Acheta domesticus*
SIZE: 3/4 to 7/8 inch (19 to 22 mm) long
HANGS OUT: Hops indoors to shelter during cold weather
FAVORITE FOODS: Plants, other insects, stored food, and fabric!
CREATURE FEATURE: The hungry house cricket loves nibbling on clothes, especially sweaty ones!

AAARRGH, GET RID OF IT!
KEEP DOORS AND WINDOWS WELL SEALED AROUND THE EDGES.

HOUSE SPIDER

LATIN NAME: *Tegenaria domestica*
SIZE: Up to 1/2 inch (12 mm) long
HANGS OUT: Ceilings, cupboards, cracks in floorboards, or any handy hiding place
FAVORITE FOOD: Other bugs
CREATURE FEATURE: The female eats the male after mating.

DON'T GET RID OF IT!
THE HELPFUL HOUSE SPIDER IS HARMLESS AND GOBBLES UP OTHER CREEPY-CRAWLIES.

DIRTY MONEY

YUCK-O-METER

EWW · GROSS · NASTY · DISGUSTING

ALL DAY LONG, CASH GETS PASSED FROM ONE PERSON TO ANOTHER. It touches lint-filled pockets, grubby purses, unwashed hands, and the insides of tills. It rolls around on dirty floors and hangs out in the cushions of couches, mingling with creepy-crawlies, cobwebs, and old crumbs. Yet a lot of the time, we don't stop to think about where our cash has been. So, some scientists decided to take a closer look at coins and banknotes to find out just how clean—or dirty!—they are. When they'd finished screaming in horror (just kidding), they reported a whole host of supergross findings …

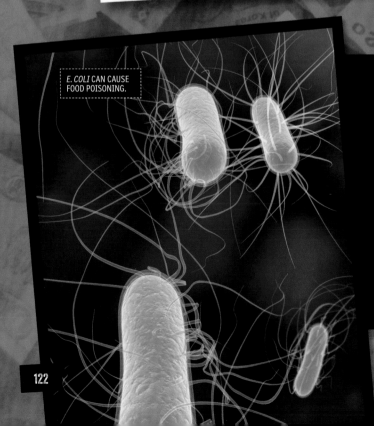

E. COLI CAN CAUSE FOOD POISONING.

GERMS

Not surprisingly, germs top the list, with thousands of species of bacteria and viruses found on notes and coins, such as:

🍀 Mouth germs from people's teeth and gums. No, you shouldn't be putting money in your mouth! But this is probably caused by people touching their mouths, then handling cash.

🍀 Acne germs, from people's faces

🍀 Food poisoning bugs, like *E. coli* and *Salmonella*

🍀 Viruses that cause colds and flu. (These can stay alive for longer if they're trapped in a smear of snot!)

FOOD

Money is often close to food. For example, when someone makes a sandwich in a café, they then take the payment for it. Or you might eat a snack like a cookie and then handle money soon afterward. The result: money covered in moldy morsels!

ANIMAL BITS

Another finding was DNA from animals—mainly pets like dogs, cats, and guinea pigs. Their hairs, skin cells, and drool end up on people's hands, and then on their cash. One scientist even found rhino DNA—maybe that money had been handled by a zookeeper!

A TYPICAL BANKNOTE CIRCULATES FOR BETWEEN THREE AND 20 YEARS, PASSING BETWEEN HUNDREDS OR SOMETIMES THOUSANDS OF DIFFERENT PEOPLE, BEFORE IT WEARS OUT.

CRAZY CURRENCY

WE'RE USED TO METAL COINS AND PAPER BANKNOTES, BUT OTHER THINGS CAN BE USED AS MONEY TOO. CHECK OUT THESE STRANGELY GROSS CURRENCIES, PAST AND PRESENT ...

STINKY CHEESE: BIG WHEELS OF LONG-LASTING PARMESAN CHEESE HAVE BEEN USED AS MONEY IN ITALY IN THE PAST. SOME BANKS STILL HOLD STOCKS OF IT TO SECURE LOANS. IT'S EVEN BEEN STOLEN BY BANK ROBBERS!

FISH: IN MEDIEVAL ICELAND, YOU COULD PAY FOR THINGS WITH DRIED FISH. PACKETS OF MACKEREL HAVE ALSO BEEN USED AS CURRENCY IN PRISONS, WHERE ACTUAL CASH IS IN SHORT SUPPLY. THIS MAY BE BECAUSE MOST PRISONERS DON'T LIKE EATING IT, SO THEY TRADE WITH IT INSTEAD!

SQUIRREL SKINS: SQUIRREL PELTS WERE A COMMON SUBSTITUTE FOR CASH IN RUSSIA AND FINLAND AROUND 900 YEARS AGO. YOU COULD EVEN PAY WITH SMALLER PARTS OF A SKIN TOO, SUCH AS A SNOUT OR PAW!

FECAL MATTER

That's poop, in non-science speak! Tiny traces of both poop and pee end up on cash, because a lot of people don't wash their hands after going to the bathroom. *Ewww!*

THE DIRTIEST DOUGH

Now you know your lucre really is filthy—but is all moolah equally disgusting? No! Scientists found that paper money is much dirtier than coins. As coins are hard and smooth, dirt rubs off them more easily. Banknotes, which can be made from paper, cloth, or sometimes plastic, have a rougher surface, with nooks and crannies that can trap dirt.

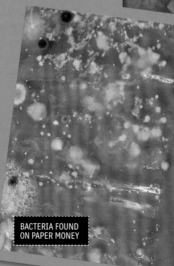

BACTERIA FOUND ON PAPER MONEY

The more a bill is used, the dirtier it will be. Lower-value bills are the grossest, as they get passed around more. For example, the cootie champion in the United States is the humble one-dollar bill.

YOU'VE GOT GAS!

UGH, WHAT'S THAT SMELL? IT DEFINITELY WASN'T US! OK, OK, you're right—whoever smelt it dealt it! Gross as it seems, gas is a completely natural part of life. Our bodies don't stop at pooping and peeing—they also release strange, stinky gas into the air. Yes, we're talking about the gas that escapes from both ends. Where does all that gas come from in the first place?

BURRRRRP!

Let's start with burps, also known as belches. They happen because, quite simply, what goes in must come out. While you are eating, you usually swallow some air along with your food. After a meal, the air collects, bubbles back up your esophagus (the tube that connects your mouth to your stomach), and escapes from your throat with that strange croaking sound.

Burps can smell bad, and that's because your stomach is a pretty stinky place. It's full of superstrong acid, which is there to break down, dissolve, and digest food. Think of what it smells like when you throw up—that's what stomach acid smells like. Combine that stench with the whiff of whatever you've been eating (like garlic bread, stinky cheese, or a tuna sandwich) and a gross-smelling burp is guaranteed!

PARDON YOU!

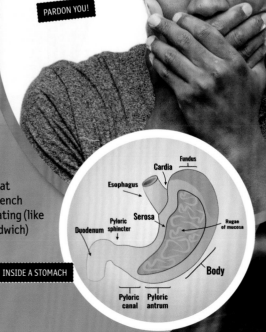

INSIDE A STOMACH

Fundus
Cardia
Esophagus
Serosa
Rugae of mucosa
Pyloric sphincter
Duodenum
Body
Pyloric canal
Pyloric antrum

THE GAS FILES: BURPING

PAUL HUNN, CHAMPION BURPER!

- It's normal to burp a few times after each meal. Burping all day long could mean you have indigestion, or you are swallowing a lot of air.

- In 2009, the U.K.'s Paul Hunn smashed the record for loudest burp. He hit a volume of 109.9 decibels—that's louder than a chain saw!

- Want to burp less? Try eating more slowly, and don't chew gum, talk while you eat, or drink with a straw—all known to give you extra gas.

LE PÉTOMANE (REAL NAME JOSEPH PUJOL) WAS A 19TH-CENTURY "FLATULIST" WHO PERFORMED A GAS-PASSING ACT ONSTAGE. HE COULD PLAY TUNES, DO IMPRESSIONS, AND BLOW OUT CANDLES FROM YARDS AWAY!

PAAAARRRP!

Now for the lower-down and even smellier type of gas, known in polite circles as "passing wind" or "flatulence" ... or tooting, pooting, or letting one rip! Most of this isn't gas that you've swallowed. Instead, it's mainly made by the bacteria that live inside your large intestine and help to break down and digest food (see page 29). As the bacteria feed, they release bubbles of gas as a waste product. The gas needs to escape ... and the way out of the large intestine is through your rear end.

You may be surprised to learn that most of this gas is not actually very stinky at all. What causes the smell are small amounts of other chemicals, especially sulfur chemicals found in some types of foods, such as cabbage. Combine this with the smell of waste, which forms in the large intestine, and you have a recipe for some real stinkers.

THE GAS FILES: PASSING GAS

- An average person passes gas around 14 times a day!

- This totals around 6 cups (1.4 L) of gas—enough to fill one small party balloon.

- Fart-causing foods include beans, dairy products, Brussels sprouts, lentils, prunes, raisins, apricots, peas, and sugary foods.

EAT THESE FOR STINKY TOOTS!

A FEAST OF STRANGE BEASTS

GROSS NASTY DISGUSTING EWW YUCK-O-METER

ARE YOU FAMILIAR WITH THE OLD NURSERY RHYME ABOUT A PIE FULL OF BIRDS?

Sing a song of sixpence, a pocketful of rye,
Four-and-twenty blackbirds, baked in a pie,
When the pie was opened, the birds began to sing …

That wouldn't happen, right? Why would you make a pie full of living blackbirds, cut it open, and let them all fly out? It's not only kind of gross, it's also not much of a pie. If you actually wanted something to eat, you'd be left with nothing but the pastry that the blackbirds had been sitting (and possibly pooping) in. So, no way could it happen.

AMAZING ENTREMETS

Guess again, because a pie containing live animals and other crazy cuisine creations did happen—and more than once! The nursery rhyme describes a kind of dinner dish called an *entremet*, which was all the rage in medieval Europe. Though they were made of real food, the point of an entremet was to create a dazzling display to impress the guests at a feast. It would be presented between the other courses (*entremet* means "between food").

The ancient Romans had similar creations as well. In their efforts to conjure up the most amazing effects, chefs came up with some recipes that were truly bizarre—and often not very appetizing. Luckily, normal dishes were served alongside, so people didn't go hungry.

DAZZLING ENTREMETS WERE POPULAR IN MEDIEVAL EUROPE.

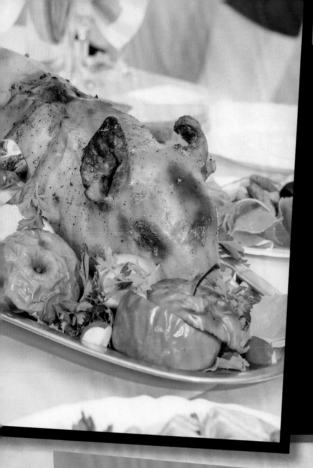

SETTING THE SCENE
The most famous entremets used food to create a scene or picture. The Coqz Heaumez was a whole chicken (complete with the head), stuffed, roasted, and dressed up as a knight, with a helmet and shield, riding on a roasted pig.

MYTHICAL BEASTS
In medieval times, you could try a slice of cockentrice, an animal that could not possibly exist, roasted and served up on the dining table. It was made by carefully sewing one end of a (deceased) rooster to the other end of a pig, cooking the resulting grotesque creation, and then covering it with spices, or even gold leaf, to hide the seams.

THE PIE IS ALIVE!
If you want to know how to make a living blackbird pie, 16th-century cookery writer Giovanni Roselli is your man. In his cookbook *Epulario*, he explains how to make an empty pie by filling it with flour as it bakes, and then cutting a hole in the base. After taking all the flour out, you pop in your blackbirds, just before serving. You didn't have to use birds—one chef made a pie full of live hopping frogs.

THE ULTIMATE
TURDUCKEN

STUFFING ONE TYPE OF MEAT INSIDE ANOTHER IS AN OLD TRADITION. TODAY WE HAVE THE TURDUCKEN, WHICH IS A CHICKEN STUFFED INTO A DUCK, STUFFED INTO A TURKEY. IN THE EARLY 1800S, THEY HAD SOMETHING A LITTLE MORE COMPLICATED: THE *RÔTI SANS PAREIL*, MEANING "ROAST WITHOUT EQUAL." IT WAS INVENTED BY A FLAMBOYANT FRENCH FOOD LOVER NAMED ALEXANDRE BALTHAZAR LAURENT GRIMOD DE LA REYNIÈRE. FROM LARGEST BIRD TO SMALLEST, THE RECIPE CALLS FOR:

1. A GIANT BUSTARD	9. A WOODCOCK
2. A TURKEY	10. A PARTRIDGE
3. A GOOSE	11. A PLOVER
4. A PHEASANT	12. A LAPWING
5. A CHICKEN	13. A QUAIL
6. A DUCK	14. A THRUSH
7. A GUINEA FOWL	15. A LARK
8. A TEAL	16. A BUNTING

... AND LAST OF ALL, A TINY GARDEN WARBLER— ALL STUFFED ONE INSIDE THE OTHER. (THE WARBLER WAS SO SMALL, NOTHING WOULD FIT INSIDE THAT EXCEPT ONE SINGLE OLIVE!)

ONLY THE BEST
FOR MY GUESTS!

When a wealthy lord or ruler threw a feast, they wanted to show off how much money they had by serving up the rarest and most exotic foods they could find, such as:

- **Flamingo tongues, ostrich, and giraffe:** Served at the most lavish Roman feasts.

- **Porpoise:** A relative of dolphins, and a favorite of medieval monarchs. Only the wealthy were allowed to eat porpoise.

- **A whole roast peacock:** After the bird was cooked, its skin and feathers would be put back on, to make the peacock look beautiful for the table. The Romans liked roast peacock, or sometimes just ate peacock brains or tongues.

- **Marigolds:** A rare vegetarian option, this pretty, edible flower was served in salads.

THE ROAST OF CHOICE FOR FANCY ROMANS

WASTE-FILLED WORLD

IMAGINE PADDLING OR SWIMMING IN A TRASH-FILLED, STINKY RIVER—OR TRYING TO WASH YOUR CLOTHES IN IT. Or even worse, having to collect your drinking water from it! Unfortunately, this is an everyday experience for people in some parts of the world, where rivers can be full of garbage, sewage, and industrial waste chemicals. Many lakes, seas, soil, and even the air we breathe are also dangerously polluted.

What Is POLLUTION?

Pollution is the name for harmful or poisonous substances that are released into the environment, making it dirty, dangerous, or (in the worst cases) deadly. It happens in all kinds of ways, but it's caused by—guess who?—yep, us humans.

Pollution isn't new; human activities have been making a mess of our planet since prehistoric times. But it wasn't so bad when there weren't many humans around. There was lots of space for everyone, and waste was eventually washed away and broken down. The enormous growth of the human population and big cities has made it much worse, as there's just too much waste for the world to deal with.

When pollution is severe, it can be a disgusting, dirty, smelly disaster. Toxic chemicals and germs spread diseases, or poison people and animals. If living things can't survive, people can't rely on fishing or crops for food.

The very worst incidents of pollution have coated cities in layers of black grime, covered oceans with oily patches many miles long, and created a mass of garbage in the Pacific.

GROSS GARBAGE is one very common type of pollution. It includes things like packaging, used diapers, old gadgets, machines, and everyday items.

ICKY INDUSTRIAL WASTE includes things like toxic dyes, harmful chemicals, and dangerous metals like mercury. They often flow out of factories into rivers or seas.

FOUL FARM RUNOFF includes fertilizers and pesticides that are used on the land and then washed into rivers and seas by rainfall.

SLIMY SEWAGE is the waste from toilets, showers, and sinks. It should be cleaned up in a water treatment plant, but not all countries have these.

THE DALDYKAN RIVER IN SIBERIA, RUSSIA, IS FLOWING BLOOD-RED HERE— PROBABLY THANKS TO WASTE CHEMICALS FROM A NICKEL-PROCESSING FACTORY.

A POLICE OFFICER IN LONDON, ENGLAND, WEARS A MASK IN THICK SMOG IN 1952.

TRAFFIC IN LONDON, ENGLAND, GROWS WORSE IN A THICK SMOG.

PEA SOUPERS Past and Present

In December 1952, a freakishly filthy disaster in London, England, killed around 10,000 people. It wasn't an attack, a flood, or an earthquake. It was smog: a yellowish, horribly deadly mixture of smoke and fog, known in those days as a "pea souper." It happened when smoke from factory chimneys and coal fires settled over the city in unusually still weather. This combined with a heavy fog to create a thick, choking cloud, which made it impossible to see. It caused traffic accidents and suffocated people and animals.

Today, burning coal has become less common in Europe, but a lot of big cities still have a seriously scary smog problem. The pollution comes from factories, power stations, and vehicle engines, and it's still a killer. Thousands of people die from asthma and other lung diseases that are triggered or made worse by the smog.

Sick From a SLICK

An oil slick is a type of pollution that happens at sea, when a tanker ship carrying crude oil (used to make gasoline, airplane fuel, and plastics) spills its cargo. The oil floats on the water for a long time before it breaks up and dissolves. Animals that feed at the sea surface, like seabirds, get coated in oil, which clogs their feathers so that they can't fly or swim. If the oil washes ashore onto coasts, it harms the wildlife there too, covering everything with horrible, thick, sludgy, sticky goop.

Luckily, there are organizations devoted to helping rescue the wildlife that is affected by oil spills and other pollution.

WHAT CAN YOU DO?

SCIENTISTS HAVE BEEN RESEARCHING TONS OF WAYS TO MAKE OUR WORLD LESS GROSS. COUNTRIES AND GOVERNMENTS ALSO NEED TO MAKE A LOT OF BIG CHANGES TO REDUCE POLLUTION (AND SOME ARE STARTING TO DO THIS). BUT THERE ARE SOME THINGS WE CAN ALL DO TO HELP TOO ...

♺ WHEREVER YOU ARE, DON'T LITTER.

♺ RECYCLE AS MUCH OF YOUR HOUSEHOLD WASTE AS YOU CAN.

♺ TAKE OLD PAINTS, GADGETS, AND BATTERIES TO A WASTE DISPOSAL CENTER TO BE RECYCLED.

♺ TRY TO SAVE ON GAS, ELECTRICITY, AND VEHICLE FUEL. TURN OFF LIGHTS YOU'RE NOT USING, WEAR A SWEATER INSTEAD OF TURNING UP THE HEAT, AND WALK OR CYCLE WHEN YOU CAN.

♺ AVOID PLASTIC BAGS AND PACKAGING, OR CHOOSE PRODUCTS WITH LESS PACKAGING.

OIL SPILLS ENDANGER SEABIRDS.

STOMACH-CHURNING SCAVENGERS

GROSS NASTY DISGUSTING EWW

YUCK-O-METER

IMAGINE IF YOUR PARENTS SAID, "HEY, WE'RE OUT OF FOOD, LET'S GO OUT AND PICK SOME UP!" Then, instead of going to the grocery store, they headed off to look for a nice bit of roadkill, or a dead animal that had been dropped by a wild eagle or mountain lion.

This probably sounds absolutely revolting, but if you were a vulture or a hyena, you'd be very happy! Animals like these are scavengers. Instead of (or sometimes in addition to) hunting and killing prey, they get their food by finishing off carrion: animals that are already dead.

VILE VULTURES

In movies and cartoons, these hunched and hulking birds are the ultimate sign of doom. Vultures circling overhead means the hero is probably toast, and the scavengers are just waiting for him or her to perish so they can tuck in. Well, if you ever see a variety of vultures overhead, fear not! In real life, vultures do fly around in big circles, because they're scanning the ground for dead animals for their next meal.

Once they locate one, the vultures fly down and jostle for position around the body buffet. Vultures have long necks and bald heads with no feathers on them. This means they can stick their heads right inside a dead animal's decaying body cavity without getting too much goop and gore caught in their feathers. They also have huge, powerful beaks for pulling and tearing away the scraps of flesh. And to top it off, their stomachs contain superstrong acid that kills all kinds of germs, so even eating something repulsively rotten doesn't make them sick.

VULTURES DEVOUR WHAT'S LEFT OF A BUFFALO.

VOMITING VULTURE

Vultures *can* throw up, though, if they want to. The turkey vulture will vomit up its rotted-meat meal, along with its powerful acidic stomach juices, as a way to put off predators who bother it or disturb its nest or chicks.

But there is a bird that's even grosser—the bald eagle. It likes vulture vomit, so it chases turkey vultures to annoy them. They barf, and the bald eagle slurps it up. *Mmmm!*

A VULTURE VOMITS UP ROTTEN MEAT FOR ITS CHICK.

NOT CONTENT WITH SIMPLY HAVING GROSS EATING HABITS, SOME VULTURES ALSO POOP DOWN THEIR OWN LEGS TO HELP THEM STAY COOL.

HYENA POOP IS WHITE, THANKS TO ALL THE CRUNCHED-UP BONES IT CONTAINS.

IF THERE'S A FIGHT OVER A CARCASS, A HYENA WILL OFTEN JUST TEAR OFF A HUGE CHUNK AND RUN AWAY WITH IT.

HEINOUS HYENAS

Hyenas are wild animals that look similar to dogs and have huge, long, powerful necks. These massive necks aren't just for looks—they're packed with muscles to give a hyena crazy crunching power. Hyenas don't turn their noses up at bones; they just rip up, crunch, and swallow them along with everything else.

These animals are also incredibly sneaky scavengers. They often wait for other hunters, such as lions or cheetahs, to bring down a tasty antelope or other prey. Then the hyenas gang up and scare the predators away from their own kill, so they can help themselves to it. Crafty!

BURYING BEETLE

CREEPY-CRAWLY CARRION-EATERS

Smaller animals can be scavengers too, like the ghoulishly gross burying beetle. During mating, a male and a female beetle team up to dig a hole beneath a dead mouse or bird, causing the carcass to fall underground. They then roll up the carcass and cover it with a special slime, released from their rear ends, that kills dangerous bacteria. Then the female lays her eggs next to the body, so that when the larvae hatch, a dead-animal feast is ready and waiting for them! If it's a bit too tough and chewy, the parents eat some themselves and then vomit it up for the hatchlings to eat. Welcome to the world, babies!

Many ants are scavengers too. If a colony of meat-eating ants finds a dead rat or lizard, they will rip chunks off to carry back to their nest until a clean skeleton is left behind.

CLEANUP CREW

SCAVENGERS' DISGUSTING DIETS MAY GROSS US OUT, BUT WE SHOULD REALLY BE THANKING THEM. CLEARING UP OLD DEAD BODIES IS ACTUALLY A VERY IMPORTANT JOB:

- VULTURES' SUPERSTRONG STOMACH ACID HELPS TO STOP THE SPREAD OF GERMS AND DISEASES THAT GROW IN ROTTING MEAT.

- BEETLES BURYING BODIES IN THE SOIL NOT ONLY TIDIES THEM UP, BUT IT ALSO ADDS NUTRIENTS TO THE SOIL, HELPING PLANTS TO GROW.

QUIZ
GROSS ANIMALS

YOU'VE ALREADY MET A FEW DISGUSTING AND GROSS ANIMALS IN THIS BOOK. But you're about to encounter a WHOLE lot more! Try your hand at this disgusting quiz to find out what kinds of revolting behavior some animals get up to.

1 RIVER-LOVING HIPPOS ARE KNOWN FOR BEING REALLY REVOLTING. THEIR HORRIBLY HEINOUS HABITS INCLUDE:

A. Spinning their tails to fling their poop in all directions

B. Letting fish nibble boogers out of their noses

C. Eating crocodile poop

D. Blowing snot bubbles

2 HOW ARE SURINAME TOAD BABIES BORN?

A. They hatch out from a big ball of saliva made by their mom.

B. Each baby is born inside a protective covering of its own poop.

C. They climb out from holes in the skin all over their mom's back.

D. They are fired out of their mom's nose at high speed.

3 WHICH DESERT ANIMAL LIKES TO PEE DOWN ITS OWN LEGS TO KEEP COOL?

A. Desert mole rat

B. Camel

C. Black fat-tailed scorpion

D. Thorny devil lizard

4 WHAT REVOLTING TACTIC DOES A SKUA USE TO GET ITSELF A FREE MEAL?

A. Sneaks up behind a seal to feed on its fishy poop

B. Nibbles chunks out of its own toes

C. Scares other seabirds until they throw up, and then eats the vomit

D. Poops on people's ice cream or fries at the seaside, so that they throw them away—and then helps itself

5 WHEN AN OPOSSUM IS IN DANGER, IT MAY PRETEND TO BE DEAD TO PUT ITS ENEMY OFF (AS SOME PREDATORS WON'T EAT DEAD PREY). HOW DOES IT PUT ON A CONVINCING ACT?

A. Pops its guts out through a hole in its stomach

B. Makes one of its legs drop off

C. Releases green slime from its butt that smells of rotting meat

D. Drips blood from its head

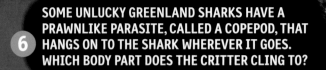

6 SOME UNLUCKY GREENLAND SHARKS HAVE A PRAWNLIKE PARASITE, CALLED A COPEPOD, THAT HANGS ON TO THE SHARK WHEREVER IT GOES. WHICH BODY PART DOES THE CRITTER CLING TO?

A. The shark's nostrils

C. The shark's eyeball

B. The shark's tongue

D. The shark's butt

7 CAECILIANS ARE WORMLIKE CREATURES RELATED TO FROGS AND TOADS. IN SOME SPECIES, THE BABIES SURVIVE BY FEEDING ON THEIR OWN MOTHER. WHICH BODY PART DO THEY EAT?

A. Her tail   B. Her eyes   C. Her brain   D. Her skin

8 DAIRY COWS PASS LOTS OF GAS FROM BOTH ENDS AS THEY CHEW GRASS. HOW MANY PARTY BALLOONS COULD ONE COW FILL WITH GAS IN HER LIFETIME?

A. 5,000

C. 115,000

B. 15,000

D. 1 million

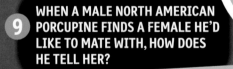

9 WHEN A MALE NORTH AMERICAN PORCUPINE FINDS A FEMALE HE'D LIKE TO MATE WITH, HOW DOES HE TELL HER?

A. He throws chunks of bear poop at her.

B. He dribbles saliva on her head.

C. He waves his butt in her face.

D. He sprays her with a stream of pee.

10 WHICH TYPE OF ANIMAL CAN SOMETIMES MAKE SPIRAL-SHAPED POOPS?

ANSWERS:

10. A) SHARKS
Some sharks have a spiral-shaped intestine, making their poop come out in the same shape.

9. D) HE SPRAYS HER WITH A STREAM OF PEE.
The female porcupine will then decide whether to accept the male as her mate, depending on how much she likes the pee's scent.

8. C) 115,000
Cows release almost as much gas as a car exhaust!

7. D) HER SKIN
Luckily, this doesn't harm the mother. She keeps regrowing the skin to keep her babies fed.

6. C) THE SHARK'S EYEBALL
The sharks don't seem to mind this too much, even though it damages their eyesight.

5. C) RELEASES GREEN SLIME FROM ITS BUTT THAT SMELLS OF ROTTING MEAT
The slime comes from the opossum's anal glands, next to its butt.

4. C) SCARES OTHER SEABIRDS UNTIL THEY THROW UP, AND THEN EATS THE VOMIT
It's the same revolting trick that bald eagles use on vultures (see page 131).

3. B) CAMEL
It's hot in the desert, and camels have very long legs!

2. C) THEY CLIMB OUT FROM HOLES IN THE SKIN ALL OVER THEIR MOM'S BACK.
If you haven't seen it, check out a video on the web. It's SO gross!

1. A) SPINNING THEIR TAILS TO FLING THEIR POOP IN ALL DIRECTIONS
Male hippos do this to mark their territory and impress females with their own special poopy smell.

HOW DID YOU DO?

1–3 CORRECT ANSWERS
Oops. You probably just couldn't believe some of those super-revolting (but correct) choices!

4–6 CORRECT ANSWERS
Not bad! You've got a pretty good idea about what's happening in the gross-animal kingdom.

7–9 CORRECT ANSWERS
You're an "atrocious animal" expert! You'd make a great zookeeper, biologist, or vet.

EXHIBITIONS OF
EWWW

GROSS
NASTY
DISGUSTING
EWW
YUCK-O-METER

YOU MIGHT THINK A TRIP TO A MUSEUM DOESN'T GET ANY MORE DISGUSTING THAN LOOKING AT SOME OLD DINOSAUR BONES. But these museums and exhibitions are different—and perfect for fans of the foul—because they'll totally gross you out! Take a tour of some of the world's most disgusting displays right here (as long as your stomach is strong enough).

Marvel at the MÜTTER MUSEUM

The Mütter Museum in Philadelphia, Pennsylvania, U.S.A., is famous for having one of the weirdest, creepiest collections of all. It's a medical museum, and it was set up after Dr. Thomas Mütter donated his huge collection of diseased body bits, surgical tools, and other curiosities to Philadelphia's College of Physicians (or medical school). There's a wide variety of truly yucky exhibits on display, including ...

A COLLECTION OF HUMAN SKULLS

WET SPECIMENS
The revoltingly named "wet specimens" are body parts preserved in jars of liquid. Check out human hands, feet, and other body parts displaying various diseases, and tumors and cysts removed from patients during operations. There's also a jar of pickled skin, and a human face that's been sliced in half so you can see what's inside. These things aren't here just to gross you out, though! Specimens like these are preserved in order to help doctors learn about diseases and recognize them when they see them.

THE AMERICAN GIANT
The most famous of over 3,000 bony bits at the museum, this is a skeleton

EINSTEIN'S BRAIN
Yes, really. Well, part of it, at least! After the great scientist Albert Einstein died in 1955, his brain was sneakily removed by a doctor who wanted to know if there was anything unusual about it. After being sliced up and preserved, some of the pieces ended up here.

PRESERVED TISSUE SUPPOSEDLY FROM THE NECK OF JOHN WILKES BOOTH, U.S. PRESIDENT ABRAHAM LINCOLN'S KILLER

IT TURNED OUT THAT EINSTEIN'S BRAIN WAS UNUSUAL! IT WAS THE SAME SIZE AND WEIGHT AS A NORMAL

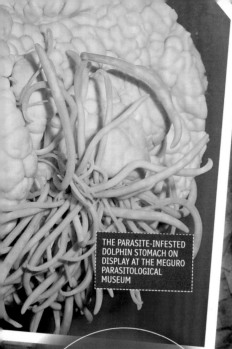

THE PARASITE-INFESTED DOLPHIN STOMACH ON DISPLAY AT THE MEGURO PARASITOLOGICAL MUSEUM

回虫 (雄)
Ascaris lumbricoides (♂)
宿主：ヒト

回虫 (雌)
Ascaris lumbricoides (♀)
宿主：ヒト

Parasite PARADE

If it can invade your body and live inside you, it's probably been preserved in a jar at the Meguro Parasitological Museum in Tokyo, Japan. This museum is small, but it has a collection of over 6,000 body-dwelling critters, with 300 of them on public display. They're mostly parasites that live in humans, but there are some from animals as well. Here you can view a dolphin's stomach full of parasitic worms, giant models of bloodsucking ticks and flies, and a ginormous 29-foot (8.8-m)-long tapeworm that was extracted from a man's intestines.

THE PARASITOLOGICAL MUSEUM ALSO HAS A SHOP, SELLING KEYCHAINS MADE OF REAL BODY PARASITES (SMALL ONES, THAT IS) ENCASED IN PLASTIC. THEY CAN BE USEFUL AFTER ALL!

WEIRD WONDERS

THERE'S GROSS, AND THEN THERE'S JUST PLAIN STRANGE! IF YOU'RE EVER IN ANY OF THESE AREAS, WHY NOT SWING BY THEIR BIZARRE MUSEUMS?

SULABH INTERNATIONAL MUSEUM OF TOILETS
TRAVEL THROUGH TOILET HISTORY AT THIS INDIAN MUSEUM, SHOWCASING EVERYTHING FROM 4,500-YEAR-OLD TOILETS OF THE ANCIENT INDUS VALLEY CIVILIZATION, RIGHT UP TO JAPAN'S MODERN TALKING TOILETS.

AVANOS HAIR MUSEUM
AVANOS, A TOWN IN TURKEY, HAS ITS OWN MUSEUM OF HAIR BELOW A POTTERY STUDIO. IT'S A COLLECTION OF HAIR SAMPLES FROM 16,000 WOMEN WHO'VE VISITED THE STUDIO, AND IT'S HOUSED IN A SERIES OF UNDERGROUND CAVES.

KANSAS BARBED WIRE MUSEUM
IF YOU'D LIKE TO FIND OUT ABOUT MORE THAN 2,000 DIFFERENT KINDS OF BARBED WIRE, STEP THIS WAY. BUT DON'T TOUCH!

A BODY WORLDS DISPLAY

MODERN Mummies

Want to come face-to-face with a mummy? What about a modern-day mummy, perfectly preserved to reveal its inner workings? If you think that sounds a bit scary, many people would agree. In 1995, body scientist Gunther von Hagens shocked the world with his first Body Worlds exhibition. He had developed a new method of preserving living things—essentially a modern method of mummification—that he called plastination. This process replaces body fluids with clear, hard plastic. There are now several Body Worlds shows around the world, including both human and animal bodies. Von Hagens receives new bodies only by donation of people who want to be preserved after their deaths. While it may
mazing feat of science, allowing visitors

ABOVE: SULABH INTERNATIONAL MUSEUM OF TOILETS

BELOW: KANSAS BARBED WIRE MUSEUM

CLEAN YOUR TEETH!

GROSS NASTY DISGUSTING
EWW XX DISGUSTING
YUCK-O-METER

IN WAS SEPTEMBER 1683, AND DUTCH CLOTH TRADESMAN ANTONIE VAN LEEUWENHOEK WAS ABOUT TO SEE SOMETHING SPECTACULAR. Using a new, superpowerful microscope that he had designed and built himself, he was taking a good look at some gloopy white tooth scrapings. He had sampled some plaque from between his own teeth, and some from other people, including two old men who said they had never cleaned their teeth in their lives.

As he stared, van Leeuwenhoek saw something MOVING in the plaque!

PLAQUE PATROL

The things van Leeuwenhoek had seen were tooth bacteria—meaning tiny animal-like creatures that live on human teeth. It was the first time anyone had discovered that humans are home to many microscopic living things, both on us and inside us.

As we now know, some types of body bacteria are helpful. But the bugs on your teeth can cause trouble. When teeth are covered in food, mouth bacteria start to feed on it. They form a "biofilm," a kind of gross layer or mat of bacteria mixed with slime, that coats the teeth. These days, we call it plaque. It's plaque that makes your teeth feel "furry" when they need a good cleaning. If you leave plaque too long, it hardens into crusty tartar, which the dentist has to scrape off.

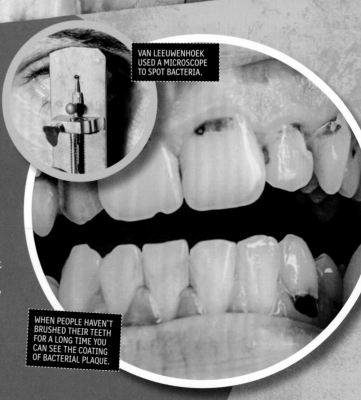

VAN LEEUWENHOEK USED A MICROSCOPE TO SPOT BACTERIA.

WHEN PEOPLE HAVEN'T BRUSHED THEIR TEETH FOR A LONG TIME YOU CAN SEE THE COATING OF BACTERIAL PLAQUE.

CREEPY CAVITIES

Those slimy bacteria aren't just gross to look at and feel with your tongue. It's a lot worse than that. As they feed, they poop out chemicals that contain strong acids. The enamel that covers and protects your teeth is super tough, but the acid can damage it by slowly dissolving and eating away at it. This can make a hole in the enamel, letting germs inside. Your tooth starts to soften and rot away—which really hurts! If it's not fixed quickly with fillings, the whole tooth might have to be pulled out.

AS TEETH DECAY, THEY BECOME BLACK AND START TO COLLAPSE.

YOUR TOOTH BACTERIA WANT YOU TO EAT THIS!

DENTAL DELIGHTS

Itching to clean your teeth yet?! Brushing your teeth at least twice a day scrubs away the plaque, bacteria, and acid, saving your teeth from a rotten, stinky fate. But why does tooth decay happen? After all, our other body parts don't fall apart if we forget to clean them ...

Part of the problem is that our teeth didn't evolve to cope with the things we eat today. Back when humans were mostly prehistoric hunter-gatherers, we didn't eat cake, candy, or breakfast cereal, or drink soda. Food meant things like meat, fish, mushrooms, and plain old river water, with a few wild berries for dessert if you were lucky. These foods didn't contain much sugar or starch, the foods that tooth bacteria love best. Now, though, we eat a lot of sugary and floury foods, giving the bacteria everything they need to go crazy.

IN THE PAST, PEOPLE DIDN'T LIVE AS LONG AS THEY DO NOW—SO THEIR TEETH DIDN'T NEED TO LAST AS LONG. WE NOW HAVE TO TAKE EXTRA CARE OF OUR TEETH.

ANCIENT TOOTH TREATMENTS

LOOKING AFTER YOUR TEETH GOES BACK A LONG WAY—ALTHOUGH SOME PEOPLE LONG AGO HAD VERY STRANGE IDEAS ABOUT WHAT WORKED ...

- THE ANCIENT EGYPTIANS MADE TOOTHBRUSHES BY CHEWING ON A STICK UNTIL THE END WAS NICE AND SOFT.

- THE ANCIENT GREEKS AND ROMANS MADE TOOTHPASTE, BUT IT DIDN'T TASTE AS GOOD AS TODAY'S. TO SCRUB THE TEETH CLEAN, THEY INCLUDED GRITTY INGREDIENTS SUCH AS GROUND-UP BONES, CRUSHED EGGSHELLS OR SEASHELLS, OR BITS OF TREE BARK OR CHARCOAL.

- ACCORDING TO ANCIENT ROMAN WRITER PLINY, A GOOD CURE FOR TOOTHACHE WAS TO CATCH A FROG BY MOONLIGHT, SPIT IN ITS MOUTH, AND TELL IT TO TAKE YOUR TOOTHACHE AWAY WITH IT.

- BECAUSE TOOTH DECAY MAKES HOLES IN TEETH, MANY PEOPLE IN THE PAST THOUGHT IT WAS CAUSED BY "TOOTH WORMS." METHODS FOR GETTING RID OF A TOOTH WORM INCLUDED FILLING THE MOUTH WITH SMOKE, OR TRYING TO TEMPT THE WORM OUT CAVITH HONEY.

ABOUT 2 PERCENT OF PEOPLE GROW EXTRA TEETH. THEY'RE USUALLY IN THE MOUTH, ALONGSIDE THE OTHER TEETH—BUT SOMETIMES THEY GROW IN PEOPLE'S NOSES, AND ONE 13-YEAR-OLD BOY FOUND A TOOTH GROWING IN HIS FOOT!

STICKY SPIDERWEBS

YUCK-O-METER

EWW · GROSS · NASTY · DISGUSTING

IMAGINE YOU'RE EXPLORING A HAUNTED HOUSE. It's dark ... it's deserted ... and as you creep through the gloom, sticky, slimy, and dusty cobwebs tangle across your face! Cobwebs are associated with all that's creepy, spooky, and scary. Besides being sticky and stringy, they might be full of dead flies, or the spider itself might still be there. Just the thought of touching a cobweb gives some people the heebie-jeebies!

Still, you don't need to be in a scary story for this to happen. Simply walk down a garden path or woodland trail, and you're just as likely to get a face full of spiderwebs. No thanks!

IN THIS VERY, VERY CLOSE-UP PIC OF A SPIDER'S REAR END, YOU CAN SEE STRANDS OF SILK EMERGING FROM THE SPIGOTS IN THE SPINNERETS.

STARTING FROM
THE BOTTOM

HOW DO SPIDERS MAKE SPIDERWEBS? WITH THEIR BUTTS!
That may sound kind of gross, but relax—the web is not made of poop. It's made of protein chemicals, collected from the food the spider eats, that are similar to human hair (although hair is not as thin or strong, and it grows *much* more slowly).

Inside their abdomens, spiders have several silk glands, where they make the spider silk in the form of a liquid. To spin it, they push it out through tiny openings on their rear ends called spinnerets. Each spinneret is made up of many even smaller openings called spigots. As the silk comes out, it hardens and dries into solid thread.

AAARRGGH! IMAGINE THE HORROR OF BEING AN INSECT UNABLE TO ESCAPE FROM A SPIDER'S STICKY TRAP.

ICKY STICKY

THOUGH YOU MIGHT NOT WANT IT IN YOUR FACE, SPIDER SILK IS AMAZING STUFF. It's incredibly thin, incredibly strong, and incredibly stretchy; the silk from some spiders can stretch up to five times its length without breaking. However, it's only sticky if the spider adds a special sticky glue onto it as it comes out. The stickiness helps the web to do its job of catching and trapping passing insects, so the spider can grab and eat them.

So if spider silk is so sticky, why don't spiders get stuck in their own webs? That's because spiders leave some parts non-sticky, so they can move around easily. They also have special nonstick claws on their feet, so they can walk on the sticky parts too if they have to.

SOME TYPES OF SPIDERS MAKE A NEW WEB EVERY DAY AND EAT THE OLD WEB TO RECYCLE THE USEFUL PROTEINS IN IT.

THIS NURSERY WEB SPIDER'S SILK "TENT" IS FULL OF BABY SPIDERS!

SUPER SILK

A SPIDER CAN MAKE SILK STRANDS OF VARYING STRENGTH, STRETCHINESS, AND THICKNESS TO DO DIFFERENT JOBS. Spiders don't use silk just for making webs—it has lots of other uses too:

SILKY STORAGE: If a spider doesn't want to eat its prey straightaway, it can bundle it up in a silk wrapping to keep it fresh for later, and stop it from escaping.

RAPPELLING ROPE: When a spider dangles from the ceiling in front of your eyes, it's reeling out silk from its spinnerets to make a rope to hang from.

STRINGY SAILS: Baby spiders spin long threads of silk, let them catch the wind, and use them to sail away through the air! This is called ballooning, and spiderlings (young spiders) do it to spread out and find new places to live.

BABY BASKETS: Some spider species make silk containers to hold their eggs or their babies. Cute!

COVERED IN COBWEBS!

SORRY TO BREAK IT TO YOU, BUT LAYERS AND LAYERS OF THICK, TANGLED COBWEBS AREN'T FOUND JUST IN OLD, ABANDONED HOUSES.

🕷 IN 2015, MILLIONS OF BALLOONING SPIDERLINGS DESCENDED ON THE TOWN OF MEMPHIS, TENNESSEE, U.S.A., COVERING HOUSES AND GARDENS WITH SILKEN THREADS.

🕷 IN 2007 AND 2015, GINORMOUS WEBS, CREATED BY MANY SPIDERS WORKING TOGETHER, APPEARED CLINGING TO TREES AND BUSHES IN TEXAS, U.S.A.

🕷 IN PAKISTAN IN 2011, SEVERE FLOODING DROVE SPIDERS FROM THE GROUND UP INTO THE TREES. BY THE TIME THE FLOODS RECEDED, THE TREES WERE COVERED IN THICK LAYERS OF WEBS.

139

YOUR FREAKY FUTURE

AS YOU'VE JUST DISCOVERED, THE WORLD AS WE KNOW IT CAN BE PRETTY GROSS. But it could be about to get a whole lot more disgusting! Scientists are hard at work on all kinds of advances in medicine, food, and technology that could make you go *ewwwww!* Good news for fans of the foul, fetid, and freaky!

Pass the POOP PILLS

The billions of bacteria living in our guts help to keep us well by fighting off other, more harmful germs. If you don't have healthy gut bugs, you can fix that by filling your guts with someone else's!

Some patients have already been given "poop pills," which really are made from other people's poop, to replace their gut bacteria after taking antibiotics. In the future, scientists think changing your gut bacteria could help with all kinds of other things too, from obesity to deadly diseases. So one day, we might all be proudly taking poop pills!

TO MAKE POOP PILLS, SCIENTISTS CLEAN UP THE HEALTHY BACTERIA FROM DONOR POOP AND PACK IT INTO CAPSULES.

THE FIRST CULTURED BURGER WAS CREATED, COOKED, AND EATEN IN 2013.

Build-a-BURGER

If you've been paying attention, you know you could be eating lots of insects in the future as the global demand for meat rises. But there's another solution for this too: "cultured" meat. This is laboratory-created meat, made by collecting a few animal cells and causing them to multiply and form a slab of meat. The first prototype cultured burgers have already been made in science labs, and eventually, cultured meat may be mass-produced. Just don't call it "Frankenmeat"—the companies that make it don't like that!

Organs to ORDER

If scientists can grow a slab of meat from cells, maybe they can grow useful body parts too? Correct! This could change the future of organ transplants. When people have a donated organ transplanted, the body often rejects it, because the cells are not its own. If you could make a new organ from your own body cells instead, it would be a perfect match.

Scientists have already figured out how to grow bladders, ears, and noses. Besides growing the cells, they have to form them into the right shape, using a "scaffold," or frame. In the future, we may be able to grow other organs too, such as stomachs, hearts, and lungs. Maybe one day people could grow themselves a whole new arm, just like a sea star does!

A SCIENTIST POSES WITH A SYNTHETIC NOSE.

A STAGE OF CRYONICS IS PRACTICED ON A DUMMY.

Keep Your HEAD!

Stored around the world right now are the frozen bodies of several hundred people who have died, but wanted to be preserved for the future. They chose to undergo a process known as "cryonics." The idea is that one day, scientific progress might make it possible to bring them back to life.

But freezing a whole body is expensive, so some people choose the cheaper option, and have their head removed and frozen on its own. Imagine waking up one day, maybe hundreds of years from now, as just a head! By then, though, there might be a way to transplant a new body onto your head, or perhaps make you a realistic robot body. Fingers crossed!

FAR, FAR INTO THE FUTURE

HUMAN BEINGS ARE STILL EVOLVING, SO SOME EXPERTS HAVE WONDERED HOW WE OURSELVES MIGHT CHANGE IN THE DISTANT FUTURE ... AND SOME OF THEIR THEORIES ARE JUST DOWNRIGHT GROSS!

FISH PEOPLE
IF SEA LEVELS KEEP RISING, WE COULD END UP WITH A VERY WATERY WORLD. BEING ABLE TO GET AROUND BY SWIMMING WOULD BE AN ADVANTAGE, SO HUMANS COULD EVOLVE WEBBED FEET AND EXTRA, SEE-THROUGH EYELIDS!

HANDY TOES
OUR LITTLE TOES ARE ALREADY MOSTLY USELESS, SO SOME SCIENTISTS THINK THEY WILL EVENTUALLY DISAPPEAR. THE BIG TOE, THOUGH, COULD GROW LONGER AND WORK MORE LIKE A THUMB, SO WE CAN HOLD MORE TOOLS, GADGETS, OR SCREENS AT ONCE!

WEAKER AND ... BENDIER?
THANKS TO MODERN TRANSPORT AND TECHNOLOGY, WE DON'T NEED TO BE AS STRONG AND RIGID AS WE ONCE DID. WE COULD END UP WITH SMALLER, WEAKER MUSCLES, AND FLEXIBLE SKELETONS, LIKE SHARKS.

PHOTO CREDITS

For Skye—A.C.

Since 1888, the National Geographic Society has
funded more than 12,000 research, exploration, and
preservation projects around the world. The Society
receives funds from National Geographic Partners, LLC,
funded in part by your purchase. A portion of the
proceeds from this book supports this vital work.
To learn more, visit natgeo.com/info.

For more information, visit nationalgeographic.com,
call 1-800-647-5463, or write to the following address:

National Geographic Partners
1145 17th Street N.W.
Washington, D.C. 20036-4688 U.S.A.

Visit us online at nationalgeographic.com/books

For librarians and teachers: ngchildrensbooks.org

More for kids from National Geographic:
natgeokids.com

National Geographic Kids magazine inspires children
to explore their world with fun yet educational
articles on animals, science, nature, and more.
Using fresh storytelling and amazing photography,
Nat Geo Kids shows kids ages 6 to 14 the fascinating
truth about the world—and why they should care.
kids.nationalgeographic.com/subscribe

For information about special discounts for bulk
purchases, please contact National Geographic Books
Special Sales: specialsales@natgeo.com

For rights or permissions inquiries, please contact
National Geographic Books Subsidiary Rights:
bookrights@natgeo.com

Designed by Project Design Group

The publisher would like to thank the following people
for making this book possible: Paige Towler, project
editor; Amanda Larsen, art director; Shannon Hibberd,
photo director; Danny Meldung, photo editor; Alix
Inchausti, production editor; Jennifer Kelly Geddes,
fact-checker; and Anne LeongSon and Gus Tello,
production assistants.

Library of Congress Cataloging-in-Publication Data

Names: Claybourne, Anna, author. | National Geographic
Kids (Firm), publisher. | National Geographic Society
(U.S.)
Title: Don't read this book before dinner!/by Anna
Claybourne. Other titles: Do not read this book before
dinner
Description: Washington, DC : National Geographic Kids,
[2019] | Audience: Ages 8-12. | Audience: Grades 4 to 6.
Identifiers: LCCN 2018032125 | ISBN 9781426334511 (pbk.)
| ISBN 9781426334528 (hardcover)
Subjects: LCSH: Food—Miscellanea—Juvenile literature.
| Food habits—Juvenile literature. | Curiosities and
wonders—Juvenile literature.
Classification: LCC TX355 .C5725 2019 | DDC 641.3—dc23
LC record available at https://lccn.loc.gov/2018032125

Printed in China
19/RRDS/1